# The First Christian Slave

# The First Christian Slave

——— Onesimus in Context ———

·

Mary Ann Beavis

FOREWORD BY
Susan Elliot

CASCADE *Books* · Eugene, Oregon

THE FIRST CHRISTIAN SLAVE
Onesimus in Context

Cascade Books
An Imprint of Wipf and Stock Publishers
199 W. 8th Ave., Suite 3
Eugene, OR 97401

www.wipfandstock.com

PAPERBACK ISBN: 978-1-7252-7018-3
HARDCOVER ISBN: 978-1-7252-7014-5
EBOOK ISBN: 978-1-7252-7019-0

*Cataloguing-in-Publication data:*

Names: Beavis, Mary Ann, author. | Elliot, Susan (Susan Margaret), foreword.

Title: The first Christian slave : Onesimus in context / by Mary Ann Beavis ; foreword by Susan Elliot.

Description: Eugene, OR: Cascade Books, 2021 | Includes bibliographical references and index.

Identifiers: ISBN 978-1-7252-7018-3 (paperback) | ISBN 978-1-7252-7014-5 (hardcover) | ISBN 978-1-7252-7019-0 (ebook)

Subjects: LCSH: Bible.—Philemon—Criticism, interpretation, etc. | Slavery—Rome—History. | Civilization, Greco-Roman.

Classification: BS2765.52 B43 2021 (print) | BS2765.52 (ebook)

01/04/21

# Contents

# Illustrations

# Foreword

IN THE OPENING STANZA of his poem, "We Wear the Mask," a child of parents who had been slaves, Paul Laurence Dunbar (1872–1908), offers a glimpse both of the experience of being enslaved and of the difficulty of understanding that experience from the standpoint of not being enslaved.

> We wear the mask that grins and lies,
> It hides our cheeks and shades our eyes, —
> This debt we pay to human guile;
> With torn and bleeding hearts we smile,
> And mouth with myriad subtleties.[1]

In order to preserve themselves at the most basic level of life or death, enslaved persons must exhibit the behaviors expected of them by their enslavers, wearing those behaviors as a mask. This is not the mask-wearing that has become a contentious issue in the United States in a pandemic. This is the mask-wearing of a continuous performance of servility and inferiority in a system of slavery. The mask is the required performance. The slaves' thoughts and all that lies within their "torn and bleeding hearts" remains mostly hidden. The clues to who they really were and are, their real thoughts, lie in the "myriad subtleties" the slaves offer as clues to their full humanity.

---

1. Dunbar, "We Wear the Mask."

Scholarly interpretations of Paul's letter to Philemon have in recent decades moved closer to listening for the voice of the "torn and bleeding heart" as well as the "myriad subtleties" of Onesimus, the slave whose fate is central to the letter. Previously scholars tended to focus on Paul's rhetorical strategy, how he was addressing Philemon, and what he was asking of him. More recently, a group of mostly African American scholars has published a ground-breaking collection of essays that begins to redirect the discussion to center Onesimus.[2] Taking the slave Onesimus as their starting point, their varied readings of the letter are informed by historical materials and slave narratives from the U.S. antebellum South. After the publication of these readings, credible scholars can no longer sideline the presence of Onesimus in interpreting the letter.

In this book, Mary Ann Beavis grapples seriously with the work these scholars have begun. Her book begins with a poignant and pointed quotation from one of the essays in the volume about the "terrible and earth-shattering silences" behind the masks of the slaves represented by Onesimus.[3] She takes up a continuation of the project of re-centering interpretation on him in a "doulocentric," or "slave-centered," reading. Her reading brings new dimensions of Onesimus's own agency to light.

Using methods of reading against the grain practiced in feminist interpretation to see the hidden and erased women, Beavis re-centers her reading on the barely visible slave members of the community and effectively employs a collection of resources to listen to the "myriad subtleties" of the evidence of the slave's own story. She employs evidence of the dynamics of slavery in the Roman empire at the time the letter was written, as most scholars do. She also slips the parameters of the first century in which New Testament scholars are often confined and incorporates later evidence of the centuries of Christian history usually considered by scholars of patristics. Evidence and narratives from the slave era in the United States provide her a means to listen more deeply for what the voice of Onesimus might say. She also reads these narratives against the

2. Johnson, Noll, and Williams, eds., *Onesimus Our Brother*.
3. Johnson, "Onesimus Speaks," 94.

grain in order to understand the masks the slaves wear when addressing their owners, showing that the slaves accomplish their own purposes in maintaining family relationships and caring for their loved ones by addressing those who enslave them with a rhetorical mask of affection. That rhetoric of affection will be familiar to scholars of Philemon, but they may never have considered that Onesimus may have had a role in constructing that rhetoric in the letter.

Beavis finds many clues to slaves' agency in general in the evidence she employs and to Onesimus's agency in Paul's letter to Philemon. She moves beyond narrow readings of Orlando Patterson's pivotal work, *Slavery and Social Death*. Some interpreters confuse Patterson's description of social death as the condition of slavery in a system as defined by slaveholders with the slaves' own view of themselves, assuming that slaves acquiesced in their status as "dead" in the social construct of slavery. Beavis instead reads the "myriad subtleties" for clues of the slaves' refusal to be socially dead, their exercising of their own agency, and their ability to take action on their own behalf. She finds abundant clues and offers an interpretation that centers on the full humanity of the slave.

The choice Beavis makes in this volume to focus on the experience and relational dynamics as she seeks to understand Onesimus as an enslaved person with agency may seem to lay aside the context of slavery as a system. Her choice of a "doulocentric" reading nevertheless addresses the system by recentering in a slave-centered "reading against the grain." She does what Walter Benjamin—the author of the brief but incisive "Theses on History" from which that phrase and concept is drawn—describes as key to changing history by changing the way history is read.[4] The key is in a choice of empathy, the question of with whom interpreters empathize. Those making claims to objectivity in historical understanding choose to empathize with the victors, the ones who control the preservation of historical memory and evidence. Those who empathize with the vanquished "brush history against the grain" to reveal other sides of the story. In a "doulocentric" reading, this means seeing, as Beavis has, the slaves, who are the spoils in the victory procession Benjamin

4. Benjamin, "Theses on the Philosophy of History," Thesis VII.

evokes in his essay, and using informed imagination to hear their voices and to see their insistence on being human beings.

Using informed imagination to read against the grain proves to be more accurate in some cases than readings that claim objectivity while empathizing with the victors. The prevailing assumption that Onesimus was a runaway, for example, was the product of what proves to have been uninformed imagination stated as fact. Using evidence from the first-century context of the letter, Beavis shows that this was an unlikely explanation for Onesimus meeting Paul in prison. The image of Onesimus as a runaway reflects empathy with slaveholding "victors" and assumes their comedic portrayals of their slaves. Her own imaginative portrayal proves more credible as an honest use of imagination well-informed.

In the conclusion of her volume, Beavis reads with this informed imagination and layers the voices of people who were enslaved in the antebellum U.S. South with her reconstruction of Onesimus's voice. In this she continues an ongoing process of reading against the grain, a process that seeks not so much to reveal objective truth as to expand understanding of unseen dimensions of an unfolding human story, dimensions of the myriad subtleties by which the silenced voices have struggled to communicate. Informed imaginative readings serve to peel back layers and help us consider possibilities. Each reading enables another. My own informed imaginative reading placed Onesimus in the web of relationships present at the reading of the letter in the household of Philemon. Just as this reading has opened new questions that Beavis takes up here, especially by exploring clues to Onesimus's agency as a human being, her reading can lead to new ways to see and hear Onesimus and all the other silenced voices in the history of the early Christ communities. For those who follow the model Beavis offers here for reading with empathy for the silenced and the erased, this volume will surely continue the process of opening deeper insight and understanding.

Susan M. (Elli) Elliott
Westar Institute

# Abbreviations

| | |
|---|---|
| BDAG | *A Greek-English Lexicon of the New Testament and Other Early Christian Literature* 3rd ed. Revised and edited by Frederick William Danker. Chicago: University of Chicago Press, 2000. |
| *Conf.* | St. Patrick, *Confessio* |
| EHV | Evangelical Heritage Version |
| *Eph.* | Ignatius, *Epistle to the Ephesians* |
| GNT | Good News Translation |
| *Gos. Phil.* | *Gospel of Philip* |
| Herm. | *Shepherd of Hermas* |
| ISV | International Standard Version |
| LCL | Loeb Classical Library |
| MEV | Modern English Version |
| NAB | New American Bible |
| NABRE | New American Bible Revised Edition |
| NIV | New International Version |
| NRSV | New Revised Standard Version |
| *Passion* | *Passion of Perpetua and Felicity* |
| *Paul and Thecla* | *Acts of Paul and Theclas* |
| *Peregrinus* | Lucian of Samosata, *The Passing of Peregrinus* |

*Perpetua and Felicity*   *Passion of Perpetua and Felicity*

*Phil.*   Ignatius, *Epistle to the Philippians*

*Smyrn.*   Ignatius, *Epistle to the Smyrnaeans*

TPT   The Passion Translation

VOICE   The Voice

# The Voice of Onesimus

Onesimus represents the terrible and earth-shattering silences, the disruptive spaces buried beneath the grand narratives of oppressive elites. Beneath these surfaces, the unintegrated voices, the trauma of histories unwritten and unworked through, remain, straining through broken sibilants, interspersed with dashes and blank spaces in the repetitive rhythms of the mad and the maddeningly marginalized to be heard. Onesimus's voice, like the unintegrated inertness of trauma, disturbs the comfort zone of the text and like a pregnant silence impinges upon our cultural and spiritual imaginations. The gravitas of the slaves' silence refracts the passing of all other light, including Paul's glowing recommendations for brotherhood and acceptance on the part of slaveholding Philemon.[1]

Truly, son, de haf has never been tol'.[2]

## The First Christian Slave

IT IS A TRUISM in popular accounts of Christian origins that the gospel appealed to marginalized persons, including women, the poor, and slaves.[3] However, as Orlando Patterson cautiously

1. Johnson, "Onesimus Speaks," 94.

2. This quotation is from Lorenzo Ivy, a former slave whose account was transcribed by Claude v. Anderson in 1937. http://www.virginiamemory.com/online-exhibitions/items/show/169, accessed November 4, 2019.

3. E.g., Kirkegaard, "Placing Early Christianity as a Social Movement,"

observed: "It is generally accepted that Christianity found many of its earliest converts among the slave populations of the Roman Empire, although the fact is surprisingly difficult to authenticate."[4] The sober assessment of Dmitris K. Kyrtatas is probably more accurate: "although most mainstream Christian leaders did not address the issue of slavery and did not make any systematic attempts to convert slaves, some few slaves found their own way to understand the Christian message and indeed the message of Jesus."[5] The presence of slaves in the *ecclesia* is presupposed in many NT and other early Christian documents, including the ancient baptismal formula: "There is no longer Jew or Greek, there is no longer slave or free, there is no longer male and female; for all of you are one in Christ Jesus" (Gal 3:28; cf. 1 Cor 12:13; Eph 6:8; Col 3:11; 1 Cor 7:21–24; 1 Tim 6:1–2; Titus 2:9–10; 1 Pet 2:18–25; *Didache* 4:13–18; *Epistle of Barnabas* 19.7; *Doctrina Apostolorum* 4.10–11). The pagan critic Celsus accused Christian teachers of directing their message to "only foolish and low individuals, and persons devoid of perception, and slaves, and women, and children" (Origen, *Contra Celsum* 3.59).[6]

Thanks to the work of feminist scholars it's relatively easy to think of the names of early women members of the *ecclesia*: Phoebe, Junia, Priscilla, Mary of Jerusalem, Tabitha, Lydia, Euodia, Syntyche, Chloe, Apphia.[7] However, the names of enslaved believers are harder to locate. Presumably, the slave girl (*paidiskō*) Rhoda (Acts 12:13–16) was a member of the church that met in

---

https://www.elca.org/JLE/Articles/619; Valentine, "Slaves in the New Testament," https://www.bibleodyssey.org/en/passages/related-articles/slavery-in-the-new-testament; Greg Carey, "Were the First Christians Rich or Poor?" https://www.huffpost.com/entry/imagining-the-first-christians-part-two_b_944019.

4. Patterson, *Slavery and Social Death*, 70.

5. Kyrtatas, "Slaves and Early Christianity," 8. However, see Troelsch, *Social Teachings of the Christian Churches*; Nock, *Early Gentile*; Carrington, *Early Christian Church*, vol. 1.

6. Quotation from *Ante-Nicene Fathers*, http://www.earlychristianwritings.com/text/celsus2.html.

7. It should be noted that any of these women could have been slaves or freedwomen.

Mary's house,[8] although as Harrill argues, in ancient literary terms her story resembles a stock scene of escapist comedy.[9] We have a few names of Christian slaves from later centuries: Euelpistos (*Martyrdom of Justin* 3), Felicitas, Revocatus, Saturninus and Secundulus (*Passion of Perpetua* 1), Sabine (*Martyrdom of Pionius*), Porphyry (*Martyrs of Palestine*), and Blandina (*Martyrs of Vienne and Lyons*). The freedman Hermas, the prophet behind the *Shepherd of Hermas*, may have been a member of a Christian household be fore his manumission. However, the one named figure almost without exception identified as an actual early Christian slave convert is Onesimus, whose name appears once in Paul's letter to Philemon (Phlm 10). Although Onesimus was likely not the first believing slave, he is the first whose name has been preserved—the first Christian slave whose name we know.

## Listening for the Voice of Onesimus

Not only is Onesimus mentioned, but he is clearly the subject of Paul's epistolary address: "I appeal to you, *on behalf of* my child, Onesimus, whom I birthed in chains" (Phlm 10).[10] He has traditionally been identified as a runaway slave, or, by some modern interpreters, as a slave sent by his master to serve the imprisoned apostle. Paul's aim in writing is notoriously difficult to discern,[11] although it's obvious that he wished Philemon to grant a vaguely worded request concerning Onesimus (Phlm 8–17), which involved, at the very least, his welcome back to the household of Philemon (Phlm 16–21): "not as a slave but more than a slave, a beloved brother" (v. 16).

---

8. On Rhoda, see Aymer, "Outrageous, Audacious, Courageous," 265–90; Charles, *Silencing of Slaves*, 133–43.

9 Harrill, *Slaves in the New Testament*, 59–66.

10. Unless otherwise indicated, all quotations of Philemon are my own translation; all other biblical quotations are from the NRSV.

11. See the discussion in Barclay, "Paul, Philemon and Christian Slave-Ownership," 161–86.

Interpreters of the letter have long been preoccupied with the question of what Paul wanted from Philemon: simply to accept an errant slave back as a "beloved brother" without punishment, to send Onesimus back to Paul for further service, or, maximally, to manumit him so that he could more effectively serve the gospel as a freedman? What Onesimus wanted from the transaction is dismissed as inaccessible through the lens of critical scholarship. As J. Albert Harrill asserts:

> Paul still treats Onesimus instrumentally, as a "thing" to be transferred, owned and used. Although we can invent stories of Onesimus that help the text seem more moral, the letter gives no hint of what Onesimus wanted or what decision he made. No matter which story of Onesimus they tell, even the most imaginative modern historians cannot restore to this Christian slave his voice or agency. There is no story that Onesimus tells. Paul considers Onesimus's wishes to be unimportant, or at least no important enough to mention to Philemon. The idea that Onesimus wanted any other life than working for Paul seems an unthinkable proposition in the letter. The slave literally is a "living tool" caught between two "masters" deciding on the use of his services.[12]

At the risk of being overly imaginative, I will question the proposition that Onesimus was merely a passive pawn in a transaction between two free men, which is just as much of a "story" as any other interpretation. At one level, this is because Onesimus was one of apparently many "Christian slaves" who became believers for reasons of their own, whose stories need to be reconstructed, admittedly, imaginatively, as is often the case with history writing. Following Carolyn Osiek and Margaret MacDonald, Marianne Bjelland Kartzow asserts that although "slaves do not figure prominently in the sources, they did, of course, also conceptualize. To understand how metaphors may have worked, we have to reimagine what kind of life stories, bodily experiences, cultural settings, memories, and narratives potentially constituted their

---

12. Harrill, *Slaves in the New Testament*, 16.

life worlds."[13] Paul does not specifically mention Onesimus's wishes, but that doesn't mean that Paul's request did not reflect his preferences, or that Onesimus was not using Paul's influence to improve his own prospects in life.

Recent scholarship has begun to focus on the involvement of slaves in the early *ecclesia*, looking for hints in the sources of the religious roles and experiences of early Christian slaves.[14] With respect specifically to Onesimus, Katherine A. Shaner probes Paul's usage of the verb *diakoneō* (Phlm 13) to refer to his protégé's "service" to him: "While this service is often interpreted as Onesimos attending to Paul's person as an enslaved person would do, the verb in this context is *diakoneō*. Related to *diakonos*, *diakoneō* denotes cultic practices rather than menial service for daily activities."[15] Susan Elli Elliott imagines the reactions of Onesimus and other slaves in Philemon's household as they listened to Paul's letter from the sidelines. For example, Onesimus might hear Paul's reference to his new "usefulness" to the community (Phlm 11) with a sense of pride in his enhanced status and belonging. Elliott observes also that his previous "uselessness" may have been a strategy used by Onesimus and other slaves to undermine their master's authority without openly defying him.[16] Onesimus's new status as Paul's valued agent might be received ambivalently: "Onesimus might feel honored in his new status as agent of the community leader, and more fully alive as others perceive him not as an object or tool but as an extension of their leader's very self. Some of the other slaves might see him as a turncoat."[17] She observes that although Paul is making a request concerning Onesimus, Onesimus has no public voice in the transaction; for the slaves in the audience, the letter might simply sound like a negotiation between masters—or they

---

13. Kartzow, *Slave Metaphor*, 4, citing Osiek and MacDonald, *A Woman's Place.*

14. For my own efforts in this regard, see Beavis, "Parable of the Slave"; Beavis, "Parable of the Talents."

15. Shaner, *Enslaved Leadership*, 58; Collins, *Diakonia*, 194, 222.

16. Elliott, *Family Empires*, 258.

17. Elliott, *Family Empires*, 254.

might suppose that Paul was petitioning Philemon for a real change in relationship.[18] A possibility not raised by Elliott is that since on his return Onesimus was a believer endorsed by the apostle Paul, his new status would have been recognized in the *ecclesia* that met in Philemon's house (whose membership likely already included slaves, freed persons, and free persons), and that he might have had a part in the discussion about his future.

This study will attempt to reconstruct a voice for Onesimus focusing on hints within and outside the text that suggest his agency and subjectivity. This is a doulocentric ("slave-centered") approach that presses beyond traditional scholarship on Philemon, which focuses on the question of what Paul wanted Philemon to do, and that represents Onesimus as a silent pawn at best, as a depraved criminal at worst. J. B. Lightfoot's oft-quoted assessment of his character took the latter approach:

> He was a thief and a runaway. His offence did not differ in any way, so far as we know, from the vulgar type of slavish offences. He seems to have done what the representative slave in the Roman comedy threatens to do, when he gets into trouble. He had "packed up some goods and taken to his heels." Rome was the natural cesspool for these offscourings of humanity. In the thronging crows of the metropolis was his best hope of secrecy. In the dregs of the city rabble he would find the society of congenial spirits.[19]

However, the centuries-long history of interpretation that represents Onesimus as a fugitive slave—by law, a criminal—returned to his owner by Paul is not supported by anything in the text of Philemon.[20] Apart from a cryptic reference to the possibility that Onesimus had somehow wronged Philemon, or owed him something (Phlm 18), there is no reason to impute criminality to

---

18. Elliott, *Family Empires*, 255.

19. Lightfoot, *Colossians and Philemon*, 310.

20. See Williams, "'No Longer as a Slave,'" 11–45; Callahan, *Embassy of Onesimus.*

him. Presumably, in Onesimus' mind, "[w]hatever the reason for Onesimus's departure, it was justified."[21]

Unfortunately, as scholars have often observed, there is very little ancient evidence of slaves', as opposed to slaveholders', perspectives on slavery.[22] A few notable exceptions are the products of literate freedmen: the philosopher Epictetus,[23] the playwright Terence,[24] the early Christian prophet Hermas (*Vis.* 1.1.1).[25] The fables of Aesop, reputedly a freedman, are another possible body of literature reflecting servile experience.[26] As I have argued elsewhere, the *Confessions* of St. Patrick—by his own account a fugitive slave—show most of the characteristics of the slave narrative genre.[27]

In contrast to the scarcity of ancient sources, there are many published narratives by emancipated slaves of eighteenth- and especially nineteenth-century North America. According to Henry Louis Gates, 204 were extant in 2014; *Barracoon*, the memoir of Cudjo Lewis (Oluale Kossola), who survived the last transatlantic slave ship, was published in 2018.[28] Additionally, there are thousands of oral histories and other relevant testimonies gathered subsequent to the U.S. Civil War.[29] These memoirs illustrate lavishly that slaves had feelings, opinions, and aspirations that contrasted with those of their enslavers; they struggled to maintain family ties, to better their prospects in life, and to maintain a sense of personal morality and integrity. They saved to purchase their own freedom, risked their lives by fleeing slavery, and planned and participated in rebellions. They had rich and varied spiritual lives. Some, like Patrick of Ireland, experienced dramatic and profound religious

21. Johnson, "Onesimus Speaks," 94.

22. See Bradley, *Slaves and Masters*, 136.

23. See Harrill, *Manumission of Slaves*, 20 n. 4.

24. Amerasingh, "Part of the Slave in Terence's Drama," 62.

25. See Beavis, "Parable of the Slave".

26. See Bradley, *Slaves and Masters*, 151–53.

27. Beavis, "Six Years a Slave." On the slave narrative genre, see Davis, ed., *Slave's Narrative*.

28. Hurston, *Barracoon*.

29. Gates, "Slave Narratives."

conversions. Some became religious ministers. There is no reason to suppose that ancient slaves did otherwise.

In this study, I will use North American slave narratives, along with other evidence, as a window into to experience of someone like Onesimus. A few comparisons of ancient and American slavery have been done,[30] but as noted earlier, little evidence of the experience of ancient slaves, religious or otherwise, is available.[31] The account below will to some extent rely on what Osiek and MacDonald call "imaginary scenes,"[32] using the slave narratives as a resource for understanding the biographies, experiences, memories, cultural settings, and stories of early Christian slaves.[33] Elliott's depiction of the reactions of the slaves in the house of Philemon to the public reading of the letter is an example of such an imaginary scene. So is Sabine Bieberstein's invocation of Apphia's role in the letter's reception:

> If we take one step further in the direction of a creative reconstruction of women's history, we can see Apphia, named at the beginning of the letter, as active in this relational network, speaking out vigorously against the structures of slavery which know only contempt for human beings and create strait-jackets from which it is almost impossible for individuals to escape. Apphia sees to it that the uncomfortable topics of justice and liberation are not overlooked, nor those without voices forgotten. If we "read the letter with Apphia's critical eyes," . . . it is possible to break open false constraints and look for liberating alternatives.[34]

Below, the perspectives and methods pioneered by feminist, African-American, and postcolonial biblical scholars will also help in

---

30. Bradley, "Engaging with Slavery," 541–42; Bradley, "Roman Slavery: Retrospect and Prospect," 482; Bradley, "Resisting Slavery at Rome," 369–70, 76. See also Dal Lago and Katsari, " Study of Ancient and Modern Slave Systems," 3–31.

31. For my previous work on this issue, see n. 14 above.

32. Osiek and MacDonald, A Woman's Place, 18–19.

33. Cf. Kartzow, Slave Metaphor, 4.

34. Bieberstein, "Disrupting the Normal Reality of Slavery," 16.

my effort to critically interrogate the rhetoric of Philemon,[35] which, like other ancient sources, "constructs (rather than describes) gender, slave/free status, economic means, and social status along traditional kyriarchal lines."[36] Rather than assuming the normativity of the kyriarchal ("lord-centered") perspective presupposed by Paul and the addresses (which comprise Philemon, Apphia, Archippus, and the *ecclesia* to which they belonged, including the new brother Onesimus), my interpretation will unabashedly seek echoes of Onesimus's voice in the text, with the understanding that the unmediated voice of the first Christian slave is as elusive as that of any other ancient figure.

## Chapter Outline

It has become axiomatic in slave studies, ancient and modern, that slaves lived in a state of social death, famously defined by Orlando Patterson as "the permanent, violent domination of natally alienated and generally dishonored persons."[37] The assertion that early Christian slaves—including Onesimus—existed in a state of social death is frequently made in the scholarship on early Christian slavery in general, and on Philemon in particular. While the notion of social death expresses something useful in describing the way that slaves and slavery have been conceptualized in many societies in disparate historical periods, it has been criticized by several scholars, and it is often mischaracterized. Chapter 1 of this study (The Agency of Onesimus) will discuss the uses and limits of the rubric of social death in understanding

---

35. E.g., Feminist studies: Bieberstein, "Disrupting the Normal Reality of Slavery," 105–16; Perkins, "Philemon," 362–63; Winter, "Philemon," 301–12; Smith, "Philemon," 605–7; Shaner, *Enslaved Leadership*, xiii–xvi, 114–15; Batten, "Philemon," 201–64; African–American studies: Johnson, Noll and Williams, eds., *Onesimus Our Brother*; Lewis, "Philemon," 437–43; Postcolonial studies: Punt, "Paul, Power and Philemon," 149–74; Lim, "Otherness of Onesimus," 215–29; Tiroyabone, "Reading Philemon in the Postcolony," 225–36.

36. Shaner, *Enslaved Leadership*, xv.

37. Patterson, *Slavery and Social Death*, 13.

slave experience in the light of evidence of the agency of slaves in different historical periods.

Chapter 2 (More Than a Slave) takes up the central theme of this study: the person and agency of Onesimus. Through doulocentric exegesis, clues in the text will be mined for Onesimus' position within the household of Philemon and his relationship to Paul, and for echoes of his voice uttered in Paul's written words. In chapter 3 (On Behalf of Onesimus), in addition to the usual ancient literary comparisons—a letter of Pliny the Elder to Sabianus on behalf of a repentant freedman, and a brief account of the intervention of Augustus in the excessively cruel punishment of a slave related by Seneca—letters from nineteenth-century slaves to their former masters will be compared to Philemon, particularly with respect to rhetorical strategies used to persuade slaveholders to comply with the wishes of the enslaved.

Chapter 4 (Begotten in Chains) considers the under-examined fact that Philemon is a prison letter, i.e., that Paul himself was a prisoner (Phlm 1, 9, 10, 13, 23)—like a slave, someone "bound against his will"[38]—at the time of writing. How would the services of someone like Onesimus be valued by someone in a vulnerable condition, fraught with anxiety and discomfort, awaiting a trial that might culminate in a death sentence? Here, the work of Elsa Tamez comparing the experience of contemporary political prisoners with the prison letter Philippians will be used to illumine Philemon.[39] Onesimus's position as an enslaved convert whose personal safety would have been compromised by his relationship to a prisoner awaiting trial will also be pondered.

Chapter 5 (The Faithful and Beloved Brother) will reopen the question of why a brief and seemingly trivial document like Philemon, with no easily discernible theological or doctrinal content and written to a recipient otherwise unattested in early Christian tradition, was preserved and ultimately included in the canon. Here, I will revisit John Knox's suggestion that the letter was preserved not primarily because of its Pauline authorship, but because of its

38 Cassidy, *Paul in Chains*, 71.

39. Tamez, "Colossians," 3–35.

association with Onesimus, remembered as an important figure in early Christianity (cf. Col 4:7–9; Ignatius, *Ephesians* 1.3; 2.1; 6.2).[40] The book will conclude with a brief, imagined memoir of Onesimus (Afterword: A Man of Inexpressible Love), interwoven with the memoirs of the formerly enslaved, ancient and modern.

40. Knox, *Philemon among the Letters of Paul.*

# 1

## The Agency of Onesimus

WITHOUT A DOUBT, THE most influential comparative study of slavery practices, both synchronically and diachronically, is Orlando Patterson's *Slavery and Social Death* (1982, 2018). It is widely cited in studies of early Christian slavery in general, and of Philemon in particular.[1] In the interpretation of Philemon, the concept of social death—understood as a state of permanent, violent domination, natal alienation, and generalized dishonor—is often invoked to bolster the claim of Onesimus' lack of voice and agency in the transaction between Paul and Philemon (or, possibly, Archippus). As the editors of *Onesimus Our Brother* put it: "Slaves have no power, no agency. According to Orlando Patterson, slaves are socially dead or they experience 'social death,' and the socially dead are not given voice. So Onesimus has remained silent in

---

1. E.g., for early Christian slavery: Harris, *Slave of Christ*, 25, 108; Martin, *Slavery as Salvation*, 228; Harrill, *Manumission of Slaves*, 14–17; *Slaves in the New Testament*, 30, 225; Glancy, *Slavery in Early Christianity*, 159, 161, 162, 171, 173; Goodrich, "From Slaves of Sin to Slaves of God," 311; Shaner, *Enslaved Leadership*, xxi; Schwaller, "Use of Slaves," 8, 16, 33, 43, 95, 104; Elliott, *Family Empires*, 233–68; Michael Flexsenhar III, *Christians in Caesar's Household*, 18. For Philemon: Barth and Blanke, *Letter to Philemon*, 330; Marchal, "Usefulness of a Onesimus," 358; Williams and Johnson, eds., *Onesimus Our Brother*, 1, 48, 58; Batten, *Philemon*, 247, 248; Punt, "Paul, Power and Philemon," 153, 155, 160; Thurston and Ryan, *Philippians & Philemon*, 169; Seesengood, *Philemon*, 48; Tolmie, ed., *Philemon in Perspective*, 117, 145, 147, 148, 149, 158, 228, 230, 232, 236, 253, 262, 264, 317.

Paul's letter to Philemon, although eerily present."[2] This perspective is reminiscent of Harrill's assertions quoted in the introduction: Onesimus' voice and agency are unrecoverable, there is no trace of his voice in the text.[3]

But is it really the case that the letter contains no hint of Onesimus' wishes for his future? Or that Onesimus, likely the bearer of the letter to its recipients in Colossae, was unaware of its contents and didn't care one way or another about Paul's request? While it is possible that Paul was preoccupied with using Onesimus as a "speaking tool" for his own purposes, I would argue that, as with other ancient documents written by the "master class," it is possible to read it against the grain in much the same way that feminist scholarship has brought early Christian women into view by interrogating "both the theoretical perspective of ancient materials and the questions that scholars bring to their materials" that "often hide women from view."[4] As Shaner observes, these insights apply to scholarship about slaves,[5] including one like Onesimus.

Shaner avoids the terminology of agency,[6] although she concedes that while ancient slaves were often forced to engage in religious activities, "we . . . cannot automatically deny slaves' ability to shape and enact religious practices"[7]—or other aspects of their lives. Indeed, her very premise that enslaved persons, including Onesimus, engaged in leadership roles in the early church implies a degree of agency,[8] although it is important to remember that sometimes these religious roles may have been imposed on them by their enslavers. With respect to Onesimus, he cannot be

---

2. Williams and Johnson, eds. *Onesimus Our Brother*, "Introduction," 1.|

3. Harrill, *Slaves in the New Testament*, 16.

4. Shaner, *Enslaved Leadership*, xiii.

5. Shaner, *Enslaved Leadership*, xiii.

6. Shaner, *Enslaved Leadership*, 126, n. 24.

7. Shaner, *Enslaved Leadership*, 149, n. 58. On forced participation in religious activities, see Peralta, "Slave Religiosity in the Roman Middle Republic," 323–29; Joshel, *Slavery in the Roman World*, 144.

8. Shaner, *Enslaved Leadership*, 53, 56–61.

assumed to have been baptized against his will,[9] by Paul or anyone else. Likely, his entry into *ecclesia* was voluntary, and undertaken for his own reasons, irrespective of Paul's intentions for him. Other aspects of Onesimus' possible role in shaping his part in the *ecclesia* will be discussed in chapter 2.

## Agency in Social Death

Patterson's concept of slavery as social death has not gone unchallenged. Vincent Brown, for example, has argued that agency is evidenced in everyday acts of survival and resistance of the enslaved.[10] In his essay "On Agency," Walter Johnson warns that the very concept of agency imports a supposedly universal, liberal notion of selfhood, marked by independence and choice, into a conversation about slavery defined by categories imposed by free white men.[11] Moreover,

> there were many ways for enslaved people to be human which it is hard to reconcile with the idea of as being "agency" *necessarily* resistant to slavery. Posing the question as a question about the condition of enslaved humanity (rather than as a search for evidence of that humanity as indexed by acts of self-determination) seems to me to open up a new way of thinking about slavery. And to invoke the idea of the condition of enslaved humanity is, for me, to try to think, at once, about the bare life existence of slaves, the ways they suffered in and resisted slavery, and the ways they flourished in slavery, not in the sense of loving their slavery, but in the sense of loving themselves and one another. To speak of "enslaved humanity" in this context is to try to imagine a

9. From at least the time of John Chrysostom (*Homilies on Philemon* 1), many commentators assume that Onesimus was baptized, presumably by Paul, although there is no reference to baptism in the letter (e.g., Winter, "Philemon," 308; Elliott, *Family Empires*, 122; Osiek, *Philippians, Philemon*, 132, 139; Thurston, *Philippians and Philemon*, 246, 251.

10. Brown, "Social Death and Political Life," 1231–49.

11. Johnson, "On Agency," 115.

history of slavery which sees the lives of enslaved people as powerfully conditioned by, though not reducible to, their slavery. For enslaved people the most basic features of their lives—feeling hungry, cold, tired, needing to go to the bathroom—revealed the extent to which even the bare life sensations of their physical bodies were sedimented with their enslavement.[12]

Rather than speaking of slave resistance, Sandra Joshel and Lauren Peterson distinguish between "strategies" and "tactics" to differentiate the calculated and institutionalized imposition of power by the dominant class (i.e., slaveholders) from the day-to-day tactics used by slaves to disrupt the order forcibly imposed by the masters.[13] Well documented tactics ranged from running away from an abusive slaveholder to more mundane strategies such as deception, pilfering, laziness, insolence, malingering, gossip, and sabotage that likely were conceived as resistant acts by the slaves who resorted to them.[14] There is ample evidence of similar behaviors among slaves in antebellum America.[15] Another tactic for which there is some evidence is philosophical or intellectual, for example, the Stoic ethos of cultivating inner freedom regardless of one's lot in life, whether free, slave, or freed.[16] As Bradley observes, "Resistance was directed towards mitigating the hardships of slavery, concerned with gaining respite and release and with damaging the interests of slave-owners, but not with changing the structure of society."[17] Studies of antebellum slavery illustrate lavishly that religion offered a source of hope and comfort for many slaves.[18] It is likely that ancient slaves' participation in

12. Johnson, "On Agency," 115. Italics original.

13. Joshel and Peterson, *Material Life of Roman Slaves*, 8–17, adopt de Certeau's distinction (*Practice of Everyday Life*).

14. Bradley, "Resisting Slavery at Rome," 373–76.

15. Feldstein, *Once a Slave*, 166–77; Blassingame, *Slave Community*, 192–22; 284–322; Escott, *Slavery Remembered*, 71–94; Raboteau, *Slave Religion*, 289–318.

16. Garnsey, *Ideas of Slavery*, 128–55.

17. Bradley, "Resisting Slavery," 381.

18. Raboteau, *Slave Religion*; Feldstein, *Once a Slave*, 75–80; Escott, *Slavery*

religious activities similarly offered them a way to "generate important elements of community, social relationships and shared humanity" that to some extent alleviated the suffering inherent in slavery.[19] As Niall McKeown remarks: "We cannot look into the hearts of the long-dead, but we must be more open to the possibility that many slaves acted as they did for primarily religious reasons, and not just to spite their masters."[20]

Social death, then, is a way of describing a set of dehumanizing conditions imposed by slaveholders on slaves, not a state of being that was unquestioningly internalized by the enslaved, or that inevitably obviated their desire to make their lives more bearable. Many slaves might have agreed with the conventional sentiment uttered by the freedman Pubilius Syrus (first century B.C.E.), that it was better to die than to endure the degradation of slavery (*Sententiae* 489). Similar sayings are found in the writings of two prominent self-emancipated slaves of the nineteenth century, both of whom fled slavery and became prominent abolitionists: Linda Brent (Harriet Jacobs),[21] and Frederick Douglass.[22] Others might have agreed with, and survived by, the pragmatic attitude expressed in two biblical passages that slavery is better than death:

> Shall we die before your eyes, both we and our land? Buy us and our land in exchange for food. We with our land will become slaves to Pharaoh; just give us seed, so that we may live and not die, and that the land may not become desolate. (Gen 47:19)

> We shall indeed become slaves, but our lives will be spared, and we shall not witness our little ones dying before our eyes, and our wives and children drawing their last breath. (Jdt 7:27)

---

*Remembered*, 110–16, 179–80; Blassingame, *Slave Community*, 131–48.

19. Hodkinson and Dick Geary, eds., *Slaves and Religions*, 1.

20. McKeown, "Magic, Religion, and the Roman Slave," 301.

21. Jacobs, *Incidents in the Life of a Slave Girl*, 96.

22. Douglass, *Narrative of the Life of Frederick Douglass*, 86.

In his retelling of the tale of the arrest of Benjamin for theft, Philo refers to enslavement as a commutation of a death sentence for their beloved youngest brother:

> Then when they were brought before the governor of the country they displayed their real affection and brotherly love with genuine feeling, for falling all together at his knees as if they were all liable to be punished for the theft, a wickedness too great to be mentioned, they all wept over him, and besought him, and gave themselves up to him, and offered to submit to voluntary slavery, and called him their master, speaking of themselves as foreign captives, as slaves, as bought with a price, and omitting no name whatever indicative of the most complete slavery; but he, wishing to try them still more, addressed them in a most angry manner, and with the greatest possible severity, and said to them, "May I never be guilty of such an action as to condemn such a number to captivity for the sin of one, for how can it be right to summon those persons to share in a punishment who have had no share in the commission of the offence? Let him alone be punished, since he alone has committed the crime. I know therefore that by your laws you condemn the man who has been found guilty of theft to be put to death in front of the city; but I, wishing to act in all respects in a gentle and most merciful manner, will mitigate the punishment, and adjudge him to slavery instead of to death." (*On Joseph* (XXXVII)[23]

This preference for enslavement, harsh and shameful though it was, rather than the finality of death, was borne out in real life by Josephus (*Ant.* 11.263; cf. *War* 3.8.7; cf. Josephus' interpretation of Esth 7:4: "she would not have troubled him [the king], if he had ordered them to be sold into bitter slavery—that would be an endurable evil—and she begged to be delivered from this fate," *Ant.* 11. 263).[24]

---

23. http://www.earlyjewishwritings.com/text/philo/book23.html, accessed November 28, 2019.

24. Quoted in Hezser, *Jewish Slavery in Antiquity*, 226.

## An Endurable Evil

Vincent Brown has rightly observed that Patterson's concept of social death is a theoretical abstraction that does not claim to describe the real-life experiences of actual enslaved persons; rather, it captures the meaning of enslavement as conceptualized by enslavers.[25] Patterson does not claim that slaves always, or even often, regarded themselves as socially dead or devoid of agency. Himself a descendant of Jamaican slaves, Patterson recognizes that the enslaved regularly resisted their oppression:

> The slave resisted his desocialization and forced service in countless ways, only one of which, rebellion, was not subtle. Against all odds he strove for some measure of regularity and predictability in his social life. Because his kin relations were illegitimate, they were all the more cherished. Because he was considered degraded, he was all the more infused with the yearning for dignity. Because of his formal isolation and liminality, he was acutely sensitive to the realities of community. The fierce love of the slave mother for her child is attested in every slaveholding society; everywhere the slave's zest for life confounded the slaveholder class; and in all slaveholding societies the existential dignity belied the slaveholder's denial of its existence.[26]

Elli Elliott is correct when she describes Patterson's work as a "comprehensive analysis of slavery as a relationship that incorporates the slaves' point of view."[27] Later, she asserts that slaves resisted the social death imposed on them by the slave system "in a variety of ways not always visible in the historical record"[28]—a conclusion amply supported in the work of Patterson and others. By his own account, Patterson was responsible for some of the earliest research that explored, in depth and in fine detail, Jamaican

25. Brown, "Social Death," 1233–34; see discussion in Bodel, "Death and Social Death in Ancient Rome," 81–108.

26. Patterson, *Slavery and Social Death*, 337–38.

27. Elliott, *Family Empires*, 21–42.

28. Elliott, *Family Empires*, 85–96.

slaves' perspectives in their sociocultural, economic, religious, funerary and familial lives,[29] and for the novel *Die the Long Day*, in which he explored "the experiences, thoughts, and feelings of Jamaican slaves" through the exercise of literary imagination.[30] As he remarks in the preface to the 2018 edition of *Slavery and Social Death*, slaves did not internalize the slaveholder ideology of social death, they saw through it.[31]

When it comes to Roman-era slaves like Onesimus, there is much less evidence of the efforts of the enslaved to assert their personhood. However, as John Bodel has observed, there are many surviving epitaphs erected by slaves to commemorate their deceased spouses and children in order to cement their tenuous families ties beyond death.[32] With their masters' permission, they joined burial associations (*collegia*) to ensure that their remains were properly interred.[33] Bodel notes that the fact that Roman slaveholders felt that it was just to respect slaves' wishes for a decent burial "indicates incidentally that slaves left informal testamentary instructions that were recognized; and it shows one way that a mixed community of slaves and free persons might assert the fundamental humanity of a dead slave by performing funerary rites for a surrogate image."[34] In fact, contrary to Franz Bömer's influential dictum that there were no *sui generis* aspects to the religion of ancient slaves,[35] Henning Wrede discovered that the type of commemorative monument that represents the divine spirit of the deceased as accompanied by a psychopomp (most often, Mercury) "was the invention of . . . newly transplanted slaves and

29. Patterson, *Slavery and Social Death*, vii–xxvi.

30. Patterson, *Slavery and Social Death*, viii, citing his novel *Die the Long Day*.

31. Patterson, *Slavery and Social Death*, xiv.

32. Bodel, "Death and Social Death," 86–89. See also Joshel, *Slavery in the Roman World*, 144–49.

33. Bodel, "Death and Social Death," 89.

34. Bodel, "Death and Social Death," 89.

35. Bömer, *Untersuchungen über die Religion der Sklaven in Griechenland und Rom*. For critique of this position, see Hodkinson and Geary, "Introduction: Slaves and Religions," 9–12. See also Peralta, "Slave Religiosity."

ex-slaves from the eastern Mediterranean, who absorbed the vo-
cabulary of traditional Roman funerary art but redeployed it with
a new grammar, creating a visual language of their own"—a kind
of private deification later adopted by others.[36]

The efforts of Roman slaves to acknowledge the divinity of
their beloved dead can be interpreted as push-back against the ontological disadvantage of the enslaved in Roman theology. According to Dan-el Padilla Peralta, a well-attested belief by the Augustan
period was that enslaved members of the household did not have
their own divine spirits, individual *genii* and *iunones*, guardian deities that belonged only to free men and women.[37] This belief was
graphically illustrated in the crossroads festival, Compitalia, which
highlighted the difference between slave and free family members:
"At this celebration, depictions of human beings were hung up on
crossroads and on altars to propitiate the Lares: free members of
the household were represented by human-like effigies, whereas
slaves were represented as mere balls."[38] Immediately after manumission, however, the freedman or woman had the opportunity to
replace the woolen ball that had previously represented them with
a human image, which, as Harriet Flower remarks, likely constituted "a moving and celebratory moment of personal transition."[39]
The belief in the spiritual inferiority of the enslaved is suggested
by the fact the spirits of slaves were sacrificed to on the Larentalia,
the feast of the collective ancestors of the Roman people, but not
at the Parentalia, when Roman families gathered at grave sites to
commemorate their kin.[40] If this kind of stark ontological distinction was known by a slave like Onesimus, baptism might have
functioned similarly, as a transition from spiritual differentiation
between slave and free to a recognition of his own, divinely recognized personhood (Gal 3:28; 1 Cor 12:13; Col 3:11; Eph 6:8).

36. Wrede, *Consecratio in Formam Deorum*, cited by Bodel, "Death and
Social Death," 88.

37. Peralta, "Slave Religiosity," 324.

38. Peralta, "Slave Religiosity," 324.

39. Flower, *Dancing Lares*, 169 (cf. Peralta, "Slave Religiosity," 331).

40. Bodel, "Death and Social Death," 95.

Bodel finds a common mythic theme of triumph over death in the transition from slavery to freed status in ancient Mediterranean cultures;[41] in real life, this was borne out in the conceptualization of the manumission of a slave as a rebirth, where the newly minted freeman acquired a patron/father.[42]

The spiritual value of American slaves was similarly denigrated in the eyes of their enslavers. The enslaved were discouraged from participating in unauthorized religious activities,[43] and anecdotes from slave narratives reveal that slaveholders taught their human chattels that they possessed lesser souls, or no souls at all:

> James Williams reports that his master told the quarters that although there was surely a hell for the slaves, there was, however, no hell for white people, who had their punishment on earth in being obliged to take care of the slaves. . . . Discouragement of religious instruction was reported by Francis Frederic to have been couched in the following language of a master: "You niggers have no souls, when you die there is an end of you, there is nothing more for you to think about than living. White people only have souls."[44] . . .

> [J. D. Green] reported that the slaveholder told the slaves that when God was making man, he made the white man out of the best clay, and the devil made the black man out of some black mud and "called him a nigger." . . . Preachers and masters reminded the slaves of the advantages they had in bondage, for when they were in their native country, they were destitute of the Bible, worshipping idols of sticks and stones, and barbarously murdering one another.[45]

> After the first rule—to obey his master—the second was to do as much work when the master or overseer was not watching as when he was. In addition to this dogma,

41. Bodel, "Death and Social Death," 97.

42. Mouritsen, *Freedman in the Roman World*, 38–39.

43. Feldstein, *Once a Slave*, 68–75; Raboteau, *Slave Religion*, 213–28.

44. Feldstein, *Once a Slave*, 69.

45. Feldstein, *Once a Slave*, 74.

said Lunsford Lane, the sermon was often preached "that it was the will of heaven from all eternity we should be slaves, and our masters be our owners."

Although some of the slaves who dictated to William C. Emerson had a concept of heaven, for the most part they were taught about this in relation to the damnation which awaited them for their disobedience. The preacher would say, "If all you niggers be good servants and obey your master and mistress you will enter the kitchen of heaven, but never into heaven."[46]

According to these testimonies, the enslaved did not accept the slaveholders' estimate of their spiritual worth, but resisted their oppressors by reinterpreting or rejecting the "white man's religion."[47] Raboteau summarizes the complexity of slave religiosity as follows:

It was otherworldly in the sense that it held that this world and this life were not the end, nor the final measure of existence. It was compensatory to the extent that it consoled and supported slaves worn out by the unremitting toil of the "peculiar institution." To conclude, however, that religion distracted slaves from concern with this life and dissuaded them from action in the present is to distort the full story and to simplify the complex role of religious motivation in human behavior. It does not always follow that belief in a future state of happiness leads to acceptance of suffering in this world.[48]

Whatever their masters, and the white preachers who worked for them, thought about the spiritual worth of the enslaved, or about the applicability of Christian teachings about justice and equality to their human chattels, slaves who heard such teachings claimed them as their own. G. W. Offley reported that his parents had taught him "that God is no respecter of persons, but gave his son to die for all, bond or free, black or white, rich or poor."[49] Although some

46. Feldstein, *Once a Slave*, 75.
47. Raboteau, *Slave Religion*, 289–318.
48. Raboteau, *Slave Religion*, 317–18.
49. Quoted in Raboteau, *Slave Religion*, 306.

slaves accepted the teachings of their oppressors that slavery was a divinely mandated institution—a position supported by some New Testament teachings (Col 3:18—4:1; Eph 5:21—6:9; cf. 1 Pet 2:18–21)—the conviction that slavery was not the will of God is common in testimonies of the formerly enslaved.[50]

## The Soul Value of Onesimus

Another way of conceptualizing the slaves' point of view is captured by the term "soul value," as coined by Daina Ramey Berry to describe the distance between the monetary value imputed to the enslaved by their enslavers, both during and after their biological lifetimes, and the human and spiritual values that the enslaved held for themselves and for each other: "their *spirit* or *soul value* . . . was an intangible marker that often defied monetization yet spoke to the spirit or soul of who they were as human beings. It represented the self-worth of enslaved people."[51] The difference between the economic worth of the enslaved and the intrinsic worth that they saw in themselves and others is illustrated by the case of Solomon Bayley, an enslaved father who laboriously saved small sums of money, first to redeem his wife, and then his son, from slavery.[52] When he heard that his son, who had been sold away to another household, was up for purchase at auction, he bid all he had, but it was not enough; fortunately, three bystanders chipped in so that he could outbid his competitor.[53] Berry imagines the scene from the son, Spence's, perspective:

> How might he have experienced this trade? What was it like to watch his father bid on him? Was he proud? Did he even remember his father? Did it matter? Here was someone who valued him in a different way. His father's actions

50. Raboteau, *Slave Religion*, 309–13.

51. Berry, *Price for Their Pound of Flesh*, 6. I am indebted to Jennifer Glancy for her mention of this work in "Bodies for Sale," SBL Annual Meeting, San Diego, November 23, 2019.

52. Berry, *Price*, 63.

53. Berry, *Price*, 64.

show a man trying to live in freedom with those dear to him. Participating in an auction for his own child signals that some enslaved people faced their commodification in the very space in which they and their families were objectified. Spence witnessed his father actively trying to purchase him so their family could life in a place where people valued him beyond their market price. His father came prepared to buy him and play by the rules of an institution that defined his family as property. The institution of slavery did not always account for soul values.[54]

Similar questions can be asked about Onesimus. Did he perceive his conception as a "child" by Paul (Phlm 10), who described him as "his own heart," as a recognition of his soul value, his intrinsic worth? As Judith M. Ryan notes, the phrase *ta ema splanchna* (Phlm 12) is "Synonymous with *kardia* (also 'heart') and *pneuma* ('spirit'), . . . a term that conveys such depth that, with this personal identification with Onesimus, Paul expresses one of the most personal bonds of love that can unite one person with another."[55] Arguably, the soul value of the enslaved is recognized in a few early Christian teachings enshrined in the NT: the pre-Pauline baptismal creed dissolving the slave/free distinction in Gal 3:28 (however unsatisfactorily it may be understood in the Galatian epistle),[56] and Rev 18:13, where the "bodies" of enslaved human beings are pointedly identified as "human souls" (*psychas anthrōpōn*). As Glancy observes, "By emphasizing that not only bodies but also souls were for sale, John implicitly condemned the practice of trading in human flesh"[57]—and affirmed the soul value of the bodies/slaves bought and sold by "the merchants of the earth." Did Onesimus respond to Paul's advocacy on his behalf as affirming his value as a human soul?

If, indeed, Paul's request on behalf of Onesimus was based on his recognition of the common humanity of slave and free in

54. Berry, *Price*, 64.

55. Ryan, *Philemon*, 236.

56. See the critique in Glancy, *Slavery in Early Christianity*, 34–38. See also Patterson, *Forgotten Creed*, 97–120.

57. Glancy, *Slavery in Early Christianity*, 85.

Christ, it is important to acknowledge that this does not imply advocacy for the wholesale abolition of slavery, or that critique of the distinction between slave and free was otherwise unknown in antiquity. The Stoic philosopher Epictetus, himself a freedman, held that corporeal slavery was irrelevant; the only true slavery was spiritual. This does not mean that he opposed institutional slavery; rather, he held that all persons, whatever their social status, should accept their divinely ordained lot in life philosophically: "Rich or poor, free or slave, each person should only care what is in the control of every person, that is, proper discernment and alignment of the will with what is right."[58] Some utopian thinkers were capable of imagining societies without slavery;[59] according to Philo and Josephus, the Essenes and the Therapeutae, both Jewish utopian communities, actually eschewed the use of slaves.[60] According to Josephus, the Essenes did not keep slaves because it tempted them to be unjust (Josephus, *Antiquities* 18.21). Philo explains that the Therapeutae regarded slavery as contrary to nature (*De Vita Contemplativa* 70), and that the Essenes regarded slaveholding as unjust and unnatural, an affront to fundamental human equality (*Quod Omnis Probus* 79). Someone like Onesimus might have admired these ideas if he heard tell of them. He might well have been attracted to the gospel by the utopian ideal held out by the ancient creed: *ouk eni doulos oude eleutheros*, no matter how imperfectly it was lived out in the *ecclesia*. But one thing that can be said with certainty about his embrace of the gospel was that he saw it as a path to improving his lot in life, materially and spiritually, and that he regarded the patronage of the apostle and the divine patron, Christ, as advantageous to his future life, in slavery or otherwise.

---

58. Glancy, *Slavery in Early Christianity*, 32.

59. See Fairey, "Slavery in the Classical Utopia."

60. Re the Therapeutae: Philo, *De Vita Contemplativa*, 70; re the Essenes: Philo, *Quod Omnis Probus Liber sit* 79; *Apologia* 11.4; Josephus, *Antiquities* 18.21.

## The Agency of a Runaway

As the next chapter will show, the ancient hypothesis that Onesimus was a fugitive slave who sought out Paul to plead with Philemon to take him back without serious repercussions is filled with implausibilities. However, it has been taken seriously by Christian interpreters since John Chrysostom,[61] and it actually presupposes a high degree of agency on the part of Onesimus. If, as Keith Bradley surmises, Roman-era slaves responded to their enslavement similarly to modes of resistance employed by New World slaves,[62] flight was a desperate and dangerous enterprise, often prompted by intolerable treatment—or simply by a strong desire for freedom. The ancient documentary evidence shows that slaves frequently ran away from their masters, who made considerable efforts to retrieve them.[63] Captured fugitives were often punished brutally, and collared or tattooed to discourage future escapes. The same holds true in the North American context. Slaves were valuable property, and slaveholders were vigilant in guarding them, and in retrieving those who fled.[64] Blassingame remarks on the extreme resourcefulness of American slaves, who carefully planned the timing of their flight, and used all kinds of subterfuges to effect their escape:

> Weekends, Christmas holidays, and the months when corn was still standing in the fields were the favorite times for running away. They mailed themselves in boxes, hid, often with the aid of black sailors or sympathetic white captains, in the holds of North-bound ships, disguised their sex, paid poor whites to write passes for them, or, when literate, wrote their own passes; they stowed away on steamboats, pretended to be loyal and so submissive that their masters took them to the North where they disappeared; or they passed for white. A limited amount of material was needed to begin their journey, but it was often crucial. A warm

61. See Callahan, *Embassy of Onesimus*, 13–16.

62. Bradley, *Slavery and Society*, 122.

63. Bradley, *Slavery and Society*, 118–21.

64. Feldstein, *Once a Slave*, 151, 154–55.

jacket, some pepper, a gun or knife, and a small cache of food (a couple of ears of corn would suffice) were essential. These could be stolen from the master.[65]

The unexpected flight of an ostensibly loyal slave, theft of supplies needed for the journey, stowing away on ships, and assistance of fugitives by freedmen, are all documented for ancient runaways.[66] Escott notes that although relatively few American slaves actually ran away due to the seeming futility of the effort, nonetheless "historians have correctly noted that it loomed large in the slaves' consciousness as a vital option, a course which always remained open if circumstances grew intolerable."[67] Likewise, a slave like Onesimus might harbor dreams of flight as a desperate bid for freedom, even if he or she never resorted to it. Actions interpreted as crimes by the slaveholder class—running away, stealing, aiding a fugitive—would have been interpreted very differently by the fugitives: as escaping from exploitation and abuse, as taking just recompense for years of unpaid labor, as acting mercifully to a refugee. From the perspective of the enslaved, running away was a bold assertion of the soul value of the self-emancipated person; as Feldman puts it: "the fugitive slave represented ultimate resistance to the system and to dehumanization."[68]

In the American context, there is evidence that a few slaves expressed their soul value by *refusing* to run away. William Grimes suffered pangs of conscience for having fled his master.[69] Josiah Henson, so trusted by his master that he worked as an overseer, eschewed the chance for his own freedom—and those of his charges—when transporting a group of slaves by boat on the Ohio River, where they "were repeatedly told . . . that [they] were no longer slaves but free men, if [they] chose to be so."[70] Henson, who

65. Blassingame, *Slave Community*, 200. See also Feldman, *Once a Slave*, 149–58.

66. Bradley, *Slavery and Society*, 118, 121.

67. Escott, *Slavery Remembered*, 82.

68. Feldman, *Once a Slave*, 149.

69. Raboteau, *Slave Religion*, 303.

70. Raboteau, *Slave Religion*, 303.

eventually realized that his loyalty to his master was misplaced and fled to Canada, came to deeply regret his decision:

> Often since that day has my soul been pierced with bitter anguish, at the thought of having been thus instrumental in consigning to the infernal bondage of slavery, so many of my fellow-beings. I have wrestled in prayer with God for forgiveness. Having experienced myself the sweetness of liberty, and knowing too well the after-misery of a number of these slaves, my infatuation has often seemed to me to have been the unpardonable sin. But I console myself with the thought that I acted according to my best light, though the light that was in me was darkness. Those were my days of ignorance. I knew not then the glory of free manhood, or that the title-deed of the slave-owner is robbery and outrage.[71]

Henson, whose reputation for moral uprightness inspired Harriet Beecher Stowe, initially postponed his freedom out of respect for his master's property rights, a position that he eventually rejected. I would add the example of an equally famous ex-slave, Elizabeth Keckley, dressmaker to Mary Todd Lincoln and other fashionable Washington ladies, who indignantly refused her master's offer to let her escape from St. Louis to the free state of Iowa with her son:

> I looked at him in astonishment, and earnestly replied: "No, master, I do not wish to be free in such a manner. If such had been my wish, I should never have troubled you about obtaining your consent to my purchasing myself. I can cross the river any day, as you well know, and have frequently done so, but will never leave you in such a manner. By the laws of the land I am your slave—you are my master, and I will only be free by such means as the laws of the country provide." He expected this answer, and I knew that he was pleased. Some time afterwards he told me that he had reconsidered the question; that I had served his family faithfully; that I deserved my freedom, and that he would take $1200 for myself and boy.[72]

71. Henson, *Autobiography of the Rev. Josiah Henson*, 48.
72. Keckley, *Behind the Scenes*, 48–49.

She eventually raised the money and purchased her freedom in 1855.[73]

Raboteau observes that many slaves rejected slaveholder morality, but a few, like Grimes, Henson, and Keckley, took pride in upholding standards of virtue superior to that of their masters. By so doing, "they developed both a sense of personal dignity and an attitude of moral superiority to their masters—an attitude that could simultaneously support compliance to the system of slavery and buttress the slave's own sense of self-esteem."[74] A believing slave like Onesimus might exert his soul value by acceding to his enslaver's property rights over his person, misguided though this might seem to contemporary readers, or even by the standards of other slaves. Raboteau offers the case of Solomon Bayley, who struggled to maintain an attitude of Christian love for his enslaver even as he was attempting to sell his wife and baby daughter: "that scripture abode with me, 'He that loveth father or mother, wife or children, more than me, is not worthy of me'; then I saw it became me to hate the sin with all my heart, but still the sinner love; but I should have fainted, if I had not looked to Jesus, the author of my faith."[75] Bayley eventually bought his own freedom, after raising funds to purchase that of his wife and son. Historical evidence shows the complexity of the effect of religious faith on the attitudes and actions of slaves: "While some sought escape in the world beyond, others saw escape on this earth as a religious quest, sanctioned and directed by divine providence. (Nor were these alternatives always contradictory.)"[76] Religion could and did motivate an array of responses to enslavement, from accommodation to revolution.

---

73. Keckley, *Behind the Scenes*, 58–60.

74. Raboteau, *Slave Religion*, 301.

75. Raboteau, *Slave Religion*, 302.

76. Raboteau, *Slave Religion*, 304.

$$2$$

# More Than a Slave

BEFORE PROCEEDING TO A doulocentric commentary on the letter about Onesimus, the thorny question of the circumstances that prompted its writing must be considered. In the last chapter, I used the traditional, and widely accepted, theory that Onesimus was a runaway slave simply to illustrate that it presupposes a high degree of agency on the part of the fugitive. However, it seems highly unlikely that a runaway slave, himself a criminal in legal terms, would seek assistance from an acquaintance himself in prison (Phlm 1, 9, 10, 13, 23). It seems more likely that Onesimus was sent to Paul—perhaps in the company of others—in order to provide him with food, clothing, and financial assistance.[1] Possibly, Philemon himself travelled with Onesimus to visit Paul, and left his slave behind to continue to provide the apostle with assistance before his trial. A slave on a long, unaccompanied journey would be a flight risk, but as Keith Bradley notes, some categories of slaves—shepherds, business agents, ships' captains, slave dealers—travelled considerable distances in carrying out the duties assigned to them.[2] Paul's reference to Onesimus as serving Paul on Philemon's behalf (*hyper sou*) in v. 13 supports this interpretation. These issues will be taken up in more detail in the commentary below.

1. For scholars who take a similar view, see Thompson and Longnecker, *Philippians and Philemon*, 156.
2. Bradley, "Roman Slavery and Roman Law," 489.

For the purposes of doulocentric exegesis, we have the advantage of several interpretations of Philemon by the enslaved or formerly enslaved. The traditional interpretation of the epistle—that Onesimus was a runaway slave sent back by Paul to his master—was well suited to the aims of American slaveholders. The white, slaveholding preacher Charles Colcock Jones recalled a sermon on Philemon where he "insisted on fidelity and obedience as Christian virtues in servants and upon the authority of Paul," which elicited strong reactions from the slaves in the audience: "some solemnly declared 'there was no such Epistle in the Bible'; others, 'that they did not care if they ever heard me preach again!' . . . There were some, too, who had strong objections against me as a Preacher, because I was a *master*, and said, 'his people have to work as well as we.'"[3] In this instance, the reaction of the enslaved audience was a clear example of a hermeneutic of suspicion that saw through the kyriocentrism of the sermon and the pro-slavery interests it served. In contrast, Anthony Burns, himself a self-emancipated slave, "wrote to the Baptist congregation in Virginia which had excommunicated him for running away, 'and gave me the same right to myself that he gave the man who stole me to himself.' St. Paul sent Onesimus back to Philemon not as a servant, Burns reminded them, but as 'a brother beloved—both in the flesh and in the Lord,' as 'both a brother-man and a brother-Christian.'"[4]

The freedman and abolitionist Olaudah Equiano held a similar opinion. In his letter to the pro-slavery Rev. Raymund Harris (1778), he insisted that Paul would never have sent Onesimus back to Philemon in order to be a "slave and private property the very time when all Christians had one heart, one mind, one spirit; and all those who had property sold it, and they had all things in common amongst them. . . . I think you have done no credit to the doctrine of Christ, in asserting that Philemon was to be received

---

3. Raboteau, *Slave Religion*, 294, quoting *Tenth Annual Report, Liberty County Association* (1845), 24–25. Italics original.

4. Smith, "Slavery and Theology," 506–7 quoting Stevens, *Anthony Burns, A History*, 282–83.

back for ever as a slave."[5] For Equiano, as for Burns, Paul's exhortation that Philemon should receive Onesimus back as a more than a slave, a beloved brother (Phlm 16), clearly meant manumission.[6] In contrast, Zilpha Elaw, a free black abolitionist preacher, was skeptical of the good faith of the slaveholding Philemon: "Oh, the abominations of slavery! Though Philemon be the proprietor, and Onesimus the slave, yet every case of slavery, however lenient its afflictions and mitigated its atrocities, indicates an oppressor and the oppression."[7] While none of these interpreters explicitly takes the part of Onesimus, they all reject the rights of the slaveholder Philemon over his person, and they identify with Onesimus insofar as they hold that the optimal response to Paul's request would be his manumission. Equiano, who bought his own freedom, contended that if Christianity had been the state religion of his time, Paul would have insisted on the abolition of such an oppressive institution[8]—as, perhaps, would Onesimus.

## Translation and Commentary

### Salutation

(1) Paul, prisoner of Christ Jesus and Timothy the brother to the beloved Philemon, also our co-worker (2), and to the sister Apphia and to the brother Archippus our fellow emissary and to the assembly in your household; (3) grace to you and peace from father-God and lord Jesus Christ.

The central figure in this letter, Onesimus, is not mentioned until v. 10. A great deal of discussion has been devoted to the significance of his name, since it was common among slaves (see comment on v. 10). But, as Shaner observes, "Few scholars

---

5. Equiano, *Interesting Narrative and Other Writings*, 338.

6. Equiano, *Interesting Narrative and Other Writings*, 338.

7. Elaw, "Memoirs of the Life of Ms. Zilpha Elaw," 98.

8. Equiano, *Interesting Narrative*, 338.

consider the slave/free status of Timothy, Apphia, Archippos, or even Philemon. . . . The assumption is often made that Onesimos and a few other unnamed persons are the only enslaved ones in the community to which the letter was written."[9] If the *ecclesia* ("assembly") that met in Philemon's house was made up of free, freed, and enslaved persons (Gal 3:28; 1 Cor 12:13; Col 3:11; Eph 6:8), then several of the named and unnamed recipients could have been enslaved. If they were freed or free persons, some of them were likely slaveholders, like Philemon himself. Since slaves could in certain instances own slaves (*vicariae*), it is possible that some were simultaneously slaves and slaveholders.[10] The enslaved persons in the *ecclesia* may have been there as attendants of their masters, or there with the permission of their masters; attendance without permission would have been risky, but not impossible. If, as scholars often assume, the household baptisms referred to in Acts (10:44–48; 16:13–17, 33; 18:8; cf. 1 Cor 1:11)[11] included enslaved members of the *oikos*,[12] the slaves in the assembly would have had varying degrees of interest in the gospel, from enthusiastic (or feigned) acceptance to resigned indifference. The enslaved and formerly enslaved members of the assembly would have experienced verbal and physical (including sexual) abuse, including whipping, shackling, and branding[13]—in some cases, at the hands of their slaveholding fellow congregants (Figure 1). Some of them would have had the experience of being sold in a public slave market like domestic animals, in some cases more than once. Like American slaves, the slaves in the *ecclesia* would have been required to listen to preaching by masters, as suggested by the NT's "authorial propensity to identify with the viewpoint

9. Shaner, *Enslaved Leadership*, 57.

10. Joshel, *Slavery in the Roman World*, 143, 193; Shaner, *Enslaved Leadership*, 57.

11. On the reference to "Chloe's people" in 1 Cor 1:11, see Charles, *Silencing of Slaves*, 66-77.

12. See discussion in Glancy, *Slavery in Early Christianity*, 46–49.

13. On the punishment of Roman slaves, see Joshel, *Slavery in the Roman World*, 119–23; Bradley, *Slaves and Masters*, 113–37.

of slaveholders,"[14] although it is possible that enslaved members might have preached or prophesied (cf. Acts 2:18). If, as is likely, slaves participated in the sacred meals celebrated by the assembly, did slaveholders wait on their slaves (cf. 1 Cor 11:17–22; Luke 12:37; Mark 10:45), or were slaves expected to serve the free members of the *ekklesia* before they ate? As Carolyn Osiek observes, "Even if at the common meal at the assembly, there was some measure of commonality, someone had to serve."[15] Even in ritual settings where free persons waited on the enslaved, the role reversal would be symbolic and temporary: slaves remained slaves, masters remained masters.

Figure 1: Roman slave shackle found at Headbourne Worthy, Hampshire

14. Glancy, *Slavery in Early Christianity*, 48. On slaveholding in early Christianity, see ibid., 47–49.

15. Osiek, "What We Do and Don't Know about Early Christian Families," 206. On slave involvement in early Christian meals, see Larsen, "Early Christian Meals and Slavery," 191–203; and Glancy, "Slaves at a Greco-Roman Banquet: A Response," 204–11.

In the case of Paul and Timothy, it is conceivable that either or both of them had freedmen—and thus slaves—among their ancestors. As Sheila Briggs has perspicaciously observed, explicit references to freed persons are conspicuously lacking in the NT,[16] but Paul's humble trade as tentmaker (Acts 18:3) suggests such a family background.[17] Sandra Joshel notes that

> at the level of small-scale artisans, slavery meant training in the trade of one's owner, where that owner was him- or herself an artisan or shopkeeper. . . . [T]he opportunities for manumission in this world of work were good, and a freed slave became what his or her ex-master was—an artisan with a shop, who often was a freed slave.[18]

From the perspective of the freeborn elite, the labor of tradespersons was considered degrading and vulgar.[19] However, inscriptional evidence indicates that freed persons "saw themselves as successful individuals who had managed to make the all-important leap from slave to free in large part thanks to their own efforts."[20] Freedmen could and did own slaves,[21] so the slaveholder Philemon might have been manumitted himself with money he had laboriously earned and saved, and have regarded his freed status with pride. Any of the other persons named in the letter (cf. Phlm 23–24) could likewise have been slaves or freedmen, or have slaves and freedmen in their family histories. Some of them, like Philemon, were slaveholders.

Although there is no explicit greeting from Onesimus himself, we cannot assume that he was not party to the writing of the letter, or that he was unaware of its contents. Onesimus's apparent silence may have been strategic—as the person in the correspondence who was best acquainted with Philemon, and who would

---

16. Briggs, "The Labor of Freedpersons Is Never Free".

17. See Lampe, *Christians at Rome*, 187.

18. Joshel, *Slavery in the Roman World*, 213.

19. Joshel, *Slavery in the Roman World*, 165.

20. Mouritsen, *Freedman in the Roman World*, 281–82

21. Joshel, *Slavery in the Roman World*, 165.

have been best situated to advise Paul as to how to intervene on his behalf. If Onesimus was a literate slave, it is possible that he was the amanuensis to whom Paul dictated the letter (cf. Phlm 19). Most commentators assume that he was the messenger who brought the letter to Philemon.

## Thanksgiving

(4) I give thanks to my God always making mention of you in my prayers, (5) hearing of the love and faith you have for Christ Jesus and toward all the holy people, (6) that your partnership in faith may come to fruition in the knowledge of all goodness within us in Christ. (7) For they have much joy and encouragement from your love, because the inmost beings of the holy people are refreshed through you, brother.

Commentators often remark on the length and warmth of Paul's thanksgiving for the "love and faith" of his spiritual brother, Philemon. He imputes the same deep emotional regard of the saints ("holy people"), including himself, for Philemon that he later expresses for Onesimus (*ta splachna tōn hagiōn anapepautai dia sou* [v. 7]; *toutestin ta ema splachna* [v. 12]; cf. v. 20). In the next chapter, I will present not only the usual comparative evidence of petitions on behalf of suppliant slaves from the Roman world, but also letters from American slaves to their former owners, dictated by them to their current masters. For the time being, I will simply note that while there are obvious differences in situation and purpose, the nineteenth-century letters have salient features in common with Philemon. One of these shared is surprisingly effusive thanksgivings and expressions of affection directed from the slave to the former master. A slave simply known as Charles began his petition with the words, "Tho I may be long obliterated from your memory, you and family and connexions are yet remembered by me with grateful feelings";[22] similarly, Vilet Lester

22. Williams, *Help Me to Find My People*, 126.

began, "My loving Miss Patsy . . . I have long bin waiting to im-brace this presant and pleasant opertunity of infolding my Seans and fealings Since I was constrained to leave my Long Loved home and friends which I can not never give my Self the Least promis of returning to."[23] It's highly unlikely that either Charles or Vilet actually cherished the kinds of fond memories and affectionate esteem for their former enslavers expressed in their letters. Both had been sold to new owners and separated from loved ones, about whom they wanted information: Charles's brother Jacob, and Vilet's daughter, "my Presus little girl."[24] Like other slaves sold away from family members, they "relied on white owners and for-mer owners to get their messages through, so in addition to the conventional platitudes of nineteenth-century letter-writing, they also knew that success in reaching family members depended on expressions of caring and concern for white owners"[25]—sincere or not. As Philemon's slave, Onesimus would know the best way to address his master in making a sensitive request—like Charles and Vilet, with fulsome statements of gratitude and fond regard. He would also know that extreme tact would be required for the request conveyed in the letter to achieve the desired results—re-sults that would have a significant impact on his future.

Paul's use of the term *koinōnia* ("partnership," vv. 6, 17; cf. Phil 4:15) is a natural way for a tradesman, writing to another trades-man, to describe the joint venture of spreading the gospel. In his study of usages of *koinōnia* and cognates in a hundred inscriptions and 370 papyri (5 BCE–7 CE), Jean Ogereau noted that in both media, "persons designated as κοινωνοί are usually understood to be tied by certain socio-economic and legal obligations. . . . Such documentary examples are indeed particularly suggestive of the way in which Paul perceived some of his collaborators to be much more than mere travelling companions, but, effectively, close as-sociates who shared in the burden of responsibilities, labour, costs,

23. Williams, *Help Me to Find My People*, 127.

24. Williams, *Help Me to Find My People*, 129.

25. Williams, *Help Me to Find My People*, 126.

and benefits of his mission."[26] Part of this sharing could well have included the services of a slave, lent by Philemon to Paul to minister to him during his imprisonment. Slaves were often used as intermediaries in business transactions (cf. 1 Sam 25:40; 2 Sam 18:29; 1 Kgs 5:1; 9:27; 2 Kgs 5:6; 1 Chr 19:2; 2 Chr 8:18; Neh 6:5; Prov 9:3; Mark 12:2, 4 and par.; Luke 14:17),[27] so it is possible that, as Harrill put it, Paul simply viewed Onesimus as a "living tool" to be used by one master or another.[28] In Roman law, a slave could be the joint property of more than one owner,[29] and perhaps this was what Paul was requesting in veiled terms. However, this does not necessarily mean that Onesimus had no preference in the matter—that being in service to Paul, whether as informally shared or jointly owned, was not more appealing to him than his work in the household of Philemon. Slaves undoubtedly made distinctions between better and worse masters,[30] and had preferences for some kinds of work over others. However, if he had manumission in mind as a future reward for faithful service, he might have preferred single ownership, since "serving two masters" (Matt 6:24) could cause legal difficulties.[31]

## Body

(8) Therefore, having much boldness to command you to what is necessary, (9) rather through love I request, that which being as Paul, an elder, now also in chains for Christ Jesus—(10) I appeal to you, on behalf of my child, Onesimus, whom I bore in chains, (11) the once useless to you but now to you and to me highly serviceable, (12) whom I have returned him to you, which is my heart; (13) whom I would have kept with me, in order that on your behalf he might serve me in the bonds

26. Ogereau, "A Survey of Κοινωνία and Its Cognates," 185.

27. Hezser, *Jewish Slavery in Antiquity*, 276–77.

28. Harrill, *Slaves in the New Testament*, 16.

29. Glancy, *Slavery in Early Christianity*, 107–8.

30. See Blassingame, *Slave Community*, 263–65.

31. Blassingame, *Slave Community*, 263–65.

> of the gospel, (14) yet apart from your judgment I do
> not wish to do anything, in order that not according
> to necessity your good [may be done] but rather vol-
> untarily; (15) for perhaps through this he is separated
> for a moment in order that you may receive him for
> ever, (16) not as a slave but more than a slave, a beloved
> brother, especially to me, how much more rather to you
> also in the flesh and in the lord.

Onesimus is named for the first and only time after the effusive thanksgiving (v. 10). In the next chapter, I will elaborate on
the phraseology of Paul's request, *parakalō se peri tou emou teknou*,
which implies that he is not merely writing "concerning," "about,"
or even "for" Onesimus, as many translations render it, but *on his
behalf*,[32] the appeal that follows is, at least from Paul's perspective,
for Onesimus' benefit. To be sure, the request may simply reflect
Paul's own opinion as to what is best for his protégé, but the possibility exists that his request expresses Onesimus' own preferences.
At the very least, Onesimus likely enjoyed more freedom of movement and sense of importance running errands and relaying messages between Paul and the local *ecclesia* than he would as a slave
in the household of Philemon.

The name Onesimus is often characterized as a typical slave
name in antiquity.[33] However, as Cadwallader observes, it was a
common Greek name in Asia Minor, and could refer to anyone from
an elite free Greek to a slave prostitute at Pompeii.[34] However, it was
extremely rare among freeborn Romans, since "it was, to Roman
ears, a name that denoted servility."[35] The name means "useful," like
other names that attributed desirable characteristics to the enslaved:
"Names like Eros (love), Fides (trust, good faith), Hilarus (cheer-
ful), or Felix (lucky) imprinted the owner's hopes or fantasies on the
slave."[36] Philemon or a previous owner might have chosen the name,

32. See references in Ryan, *Philemon*, 234.

33. E.g., Batten, *Philemon*, 245.

34. Cadwallader, "Onesimus and the World of Philemon," 594.

35. Cadwallader, "Onesimus and the World of Philemon," 594.

36. Joshel, *Slavery in the Roman World*, 95.

as it suited him (cf. Varro, *The Latin Language* 8.21).[37] Although the assumption that Onesimus was a literal slave has occasionally been questioned,[38] his name together with the reference to him as a slave (*doulos*) in v. 16 seems probative.

Apart from the fact that he was enslaved, there are many things we don't know about Onesimus. How old was he? Was he homeborn or purchased? Did he have family members in Philemon's household, or elsewhere? What kinds of work did he do for Philemon? What kinds of services did he provide for Paul? We know nothing about his ethnic background, or his religiosity prior to his relationship with Paul. We can make some educated guesses about some of these matters. Since life expectancy for Roman slaves was low (17.2 years for men and 17.9 for women)[39]—perhaps several years longer in the provinces—Onesimus was likely relatively young (compared to the "elder" Paul, v. 18). Perhaps this is one of the reasons Paul refers to him as his "child" (*teknon*) (v. 10). He would have been in good enough health to make the journey from Colossae to Ephesus: "120 miles (193 km) and a six-day walking distance."[40] In general, homeborn slaves were more trusted than those purchased from abroad, and a domestic slave would be more likely to be entrusted to undertake such a journey and to be lent to Paul in order to serve him—with or without accompaniment. Onesimus was a slave in a believing household, where an assembly of believers met on a regular basis (Phlm 1). By the time he met Paul, he had likely experienced the kinds of treatment accorded to slaves mentioned earlier: verbal, physical, and sexual abuse, family separation, spiritual degradation, either personally or as inflicted on fellow slaves.

One thing we do know incontrovertibly about Onesimus is that he had, at some point, deliberately embraced the religion

37. Joshel, *Slavery in the Roman World*, 94–95.

38. E.g., Barnes, *An Inquiry into the Scriptural Views of Slavery*, 321–23; Callahan, *Embassy of Onesimus*; Seesengood, *Philemon*, 35–38.

39. Harper, "Slaves and Freedmen in Imperial Rome," 341–42.

40. Cadwallader, "Onesimus and the Social and Geographical World of Philemon," 590–604.

practiced in the household of Philemon. There are many pragmatic reasons for such a conversion, none of which are mutually exclusive. As part of a believing household, he might have initially been baptized with or without his consent or understanding. In Roman households, religion was a family matter; Stanley Stowers explains that "allowing various roles of participation according to one's place in the hierarchy of the oikos is precisely how the household cult helped maintain the order of the household. In regard to religion, the kurios was kurios because the cult belonged to him and inherited from his father because he served as 'priest.' Slaves served as slaves during the sacrifices."[41] He might have hoped that he would receive better treatment from the free members of the household if he embraced their religion eagerly— even that it might enhance his chances of eventual manumission. There is evidence that some early Christian congregations pooled their resources to pay for the manumission of enslaved members (*Herm. Sim.* 1.8; *Herm. Mand.* 8.10; Ignatius, *Pol.* 4.3; *Apostolic Constitutions* 4.9.2; 2.62.4; cf. 5.1–2; Patrick, *Letter to the Soldiers of Coroticus* 14),[42] but no such practice seems to be at issue here. However, if Onesimus' contact with Paul was instrumental in his conversion, he might have hoped that his service to a respected— and, as a prisoner, vulnerable—spiritual leader might be to his material advantage. If, as Shaner argues, slaves sometimes took on "leadership" roles in the *ecclesia*,[43] he might have hoped to gain some prestige through spiritual service (cf. v. 13)—a claim on honor by a fundamentally dishonored person. As suggested in the last chapter, the *ecclesia*'s recognition of Onesimus' soul value— his intrinsic spiritual worth—might have motivated him, much as it did African-American slaves:

> When the narrators spoke of their conversion as a re-birth, of being made entirely new, of being filled with love for everything and everybody, they revealed the depth of

41. Stowers, "A Cult from Philadelphia," 274. See also Joshel, *Slavery in the Roman World*, 144–46.

42. Harrill, *Manumission of Slaves*, 178–82.

43. Shaner, *Enslaved Leadership*, 42–62, 87–110.

internal transformation that defined their identity and self-worth. For slaves facing the dehumanizing conditions of enslavement, the daily physical, psychological, and emotional attacks against their dignity as persons, to experience the total acceptance and affirmation of themselves by God contradicted at a fundamental level the force of the very system bent on denigrating their humanity. . . . [They knew] that they were of infinite value as children of God, chosen from eternity to be saved.[44]

For the enslaved, "the experience of conversion rooted deep within the slave converts' psyche a sense of personal value and individual importance that helped to ground their identity in the unimpeachable authority of almighty God."[45]

Paul's statement that he had given birth to (or begotten) Onesimus while in prison ("in chains") (v. 10) is, as noted earlier, often interpreted as a reference to baptism, but it is difficult to see how Paul could have baptized him, or anyone, in the confines of a Roman prison (see chapter 4). As suggested above, he might have been baptized before his association with the prisoner Paul, more or less voluntarily. If Onesimus was baptized in Ephesus, it would likely have been in the setting of the Ephesian *ecclesia*, not in a prison. As Osiek surmises, Paul's language of engendering Onesimus as his "child" could also refer to a post-baptismal experience:

> it is possible that some other kind of conversion is meant, in which Onesimus acquired as new spiritual élan and identity, perhaps discovery of an apostolic vocation or a willingness to return home and face the consequences of less-than-ideal behavior.[46]

Another possibility is that the Colossian *ecclesia* practiced what Lewis Blagdon refers to as "exclusionary *koinōnia*," in which enslaved persons were deemed unworthy of baptism,[47] a practice that Paul firmly rejects in the letter. Paul uses the term *teknon*

44. Raboteau, "Introduction," *God Struck Me Dead*, xxv.

45. Raboteau, "Introduction," *God Struck Me Dead*, xxv.

46. Osiek, *Philippians and Philemon*, 135.

47. Brogdon, *Companion to Philemon*, 60–93.

("child") to refer to those whose faith he has fostered as their spiritual parent elsewhere (1 Cor 14:14–15; 2 Cor 6:13; 12:14–15; Phil 2:22; 1 Thess 2:11). Adult slaves were often referred to demeaningly as "boys/girls" (*pais, paidiskon/ō, puer, puella*), but slaves where not referred to as *tekna*.[48] Of particular interest here are Paul's references to Timothy using this terminology (Phil 2:22; 1 Cor 4:17), since, as Osiek notes, "Everything we know about Timothy indicates that the two of them got along very well together and that Paul held him in great affection and esteem. In spite of the fact that Timothy 'works for' Paul in the sense that Paul can send him on various missions, Paul sees Timothy as a 'soul friend.'"[49] Although in Philippians Paul insists that there is no one like his *isopsychos* Timothy (Phil 2:15), Paul's reference to Onesimus as "my inner being" (*ta ema splanchna*, Phlm 12) together with the identification of him as his *teknon* may indicate that Paul wanted Onesimus, like Timothy—and Philemon, for that matter (Phlm 7)—to serve with him in spreading the gospel (Phil 2:22).

The service proffered to Paul by Onesimus "in the chains of the gospel" (v. 13) is referred to by the verb *diakonē*, related to the nouns *diakonos* ("deacon") and *diakonia* ("diaconal service"). Shaner interprets this usage as a technical term for specifically cultic labor, noting that it applies not only to the Christ-cult but to cultic officiants for several Ephesian deities.[50] Thus, the "service" rendered by Onesimus was not simply a matter of waiting on Paul, but a specialized set of practices that Onesimus was trained in while in Ephesus: "Thus, the purpose clause in verse 13 . . . does not suggest that Onesimos attends to Paul's person during Paul's imprisonment. Rather, Onesimos attends to the practices of an *ekklésia* in Ephesos, which claims an imprisoned member, Paul."[51] While Shaner may overly maximize the meaning of a verb that could simply refer to the work expected of a slave (or, admittedly, the cultic service expected of a minister), she is not alone

48. Artz-Grabner, *Philemon*, 216–24.
49. Artz-Grabner, *Philemon*, 76, commenting on Phil 2:22.
50. Shaner, *Enslaved Leadership*, 68.
51. Shaner, *Enslaved Leadership*, 68.

in suggesting that Onesimus' *diakonia* was more than simply running errands for Paul: "In Christian literature the language of *diakonia* most often has to do with some kind of ministry, perhaps that of preaching or consoling. It seems then at Onesimos' conversion and baptism, a promising possible path had opened up before him, that of laboring in the ministry side by side with Paul."[52] We know from Pliny the Younger's letter to Trajan (10.96.8), where he reports on his arrest of two Christian women slaves (*ancillae*) who were called *ministrae* ("deaconesses") that diaconal service and enslavement were not mutually exclusive. On this interpretation, it could be asserted that Onesimus was not only the first (named) Christian slave, but an early instance of a named deacon (cf. Rom 16:1; Col 1:7; 4:7). However, Paul reminds Philemon that Onesimus' service is on his behalf (*hyper sou*, v. 13), a reminder that the slave's function is to represent his master—and a strong indication that Onesimus was lent out to Paul to assist him during his imprisonment. But Paul's reminder that Onesimus is there in his master's place may be a veiled dig at Philemon, who is *not* there to support Paul in his time of need.[53]

Paul's pun on Onesimus' name in v. 11 ("the one once useless to you but now to you and to me highly serviceable") has received a great deal of comment (cf. v. 20, where Paul uses the related verb *oinēmen* to refer to his wish to benefit from his relationship with Philemon).[54] Some scholars hold that the reference upholds the runaway slave hypothesis, since it's unlikely that Philemon would send Paul a "useless" slave to serve him. Rather than punning on the actual word *onēsimos* ("useful" or "profitable") he uses the synonym *chrēstos* and its opposite *achrēstos*, which, as Osiek notes, would have been pronounced exactly like "Christ" (*christos*)—rendering Onesimus "the one without Christ to you but now to you and to me very much with Christ."[55] Paul may have heard Philemon refer

52. Osiek, *Philippians and Philemon*, 137–38. See also Collins, *Diakonia*, 222.

53. Cf. Osiek, *Philippians and Philemon*, 138.

54. See discussion in Osiek, *Philippians and Philemon*, 141.

55. Osiek, *Philippians and Philemon*, 136. Cf. Suetonius, *Claudius* 25.4.

to his slave as "useless," an example of the verbal abuse Onesimus would have been subjected to at the whim of his master—not necessarily a reflection of his actual skill as a servant. Laziness ("uselessness") was a common stereotype applied to slaves in ancient and American contexts.[56] An idea of the kinds of insults casually doled out to slaves is provided by Petronius' *Satyricon*, which, as Keith Bradley notes, may be a work of satire, but nonetheless is not unrealistic when it comes to the treatment of the enslaved.[57] In the course of the work, the various *servi* are referred to as "stinking" (34), "withered," "blear-eyed" and "repulsive" (28, 64), "stand-a-gapes" (37), "wretched" (69), "officious" (74), "damned" (96), and "worthless" (30, 116)[58]—to cite a few examples. At time of writing, Onesimus may have been "useless" to Philemon simply because he was serving Paul, not his legal master—and because Philemon wanted him back. If Onesimus was the scribe who took down the letter (cf. v. 19), or simply was nearby as the letter was being dictated, he might have resented Paul's thoughtless witticism, although it was softened by the reference to his "Christian" usefulness. Joseph Marchal's suggestion that Paul's language of the utility of Onesimus might refer to the sexual use of the enslaved that was endemic in Greco-Roman culture is a worthwhile reminder that slaves—including those in Christian households[59]—were subject to sexual abuse by their enslavers and their associates.[60] However, the christological resonance of the term *chrēstos*, combined with Paul's disdain for sexual relations with (likely enslaved) prostitutes in 1 Cor 6:16–20 ("Do you not know that your bodies are members of Christ himself? Shall I then take the members of Christ and

56. Harper, *Slavery in the Late Roman World,* 253. Blassingame, *Slave Community,* 223–33.

57. Bradley, "Bitter Chain of Slavery," http://nrs.harvard.edu/urn-3:hlnc.essay:BradleyK.The_Bitter_Chain_of_Slavery.2005.

58. Arbiter, *Satyricon, Complete,* https://www.gutenberg.org/files/5225/5225-h/5225-h.htm#linkp070.0.

59. See MacDonald, "Slavery, Sexuality and House Churches," 94–113; Glancy, *Slavery in Early Christianity,* 49–53; and Glancy, "Sexual Use of Slaves," 215–29.

60. Marchal, "Usefulness of Onesimus."

unite them with a prostitute? Never!" v. 15),[61] makes it unlikely that Paul is making a coarse joke about the sharing of Onesimus' body. We cannot discount the possibility, however, that Onesimus had been sexually assaulted in the household of Philemon or a previous master in his lifetime.

The warm regard held by Paul for Onesimus (vv. 10–12) may have been completely one-sided, or gratefully reciprocated—the letter gives us no hint of Onesimus' feelings for his self-appointed spiritual father. There is evidence that some ancient slaveholders felt strong affection for favorite slaves and were willing to devote care and money to preserve their health and welfare.[62] For example,

> Cicero and his family loved Cicero's secretary Tiro and greeted his manumission with joy. Pliny the younger worried about the illness of his slaves and mourned their deaths (*Letters* 8.16; 8.19). He fretted about his slave reader Encolpius when dust cause him to spit up blood. He insisted he stop his literary activities and placed him in the care of doctors.[63]

Pliny believed that Enclopius' feelings mirrored him own (*Letters* 8.1), but, as Joshel warns, these elite Roman authors "give us only one side of the relationship, and we can at least wonder about the other side. They may have accurately recounted the feelings and behavior of their slaves and freedmen; however, these slaveholders imagined that their valued slaves shared their owners' experience."[64] Onesimus' feelings about Paul may have been as fervently held as Paul's for him, or he may have felt quite differently. We know from the American slave narratives that dissembling was a frequently used tactic:

> The slaves dissembled, they feigned ignorance and humility. . . . The slave frequently pretended to be much more humble than he actually was. When Jermain

61. It should be noted that Paul expressed no interest in the moral, physical, or spiritual welfare of the enslaved prostitutes concerned.

62. Joshel, *Slavery in the Roman World*, 188–89.

63. Joshel, *Slavery in the Roman World*, 189.

64. Joshel, *Slavery in the Roman World*, 189–90.

Loguen returned after an absence of several months to his rather despicable master, for example, he pretended to be happy. He wrote that he "went through the ceremony of servile bows and counterfeit smile to his master and mistress, and other false expressions of gladness."[65]

Onesimus would have been well practiced at giving the "master" what he wanted and saying what was expected of him. That said, the regard of some masters for their slaves could lead to manumission,[66] although it was not in Paul's power to grant it. Presumably, Onesimus would have preferred to be associated with someone who expressed deep affection for him, whether slave or freed, as opposed to someone who called him "useless" and accused him of wrongdoing (v. 18)—if indeed Philemon and not Paul was the source of these insults. American slaves recognized that some masters were better than others, and occasionally expressed genuine regard for them post-slavery.[67] Blassingame notes that in the slave narratives:

> A majority of the slaves, at one time, had one or two masters whom they considered kindly men. Josiah Henson described his mater as a "kind-hearted, liberal, and jovial" man. Grimes felt that Dr. Collock of Savannah "was the best and most humane man I ever lived with, or worked under." Isaac Jefferson recalled that his master, Thomas Jefferson, was of a similar stripe: "Old master [was] kind to servants." Elijah Marrs declared: "Our master was not hard on us." The slaveholders earned these economiums in various ways. Sparing use of the lash, provision of adequate shelter, and maintenance of the family unit all led the slaves to think of their masters as kindly men.[68]

---

65. Blassingame, *Slave Community*, 313–14; see also Feldstein, *Once a Slave*, 170–71.

66. Joshel, *Slavery in the Roman World*, 189.

67. Escott, *Slavery Remembered*, 20–22; see also Blassingame, *Slave Community*, 290–93.

68. Blassingame, *Slave Community*, 264.

Most often, however, they recognized that even the most benevolent masters were motivated by self-interest.[69]

## Recapitulation

> (17) Since you are in partnership with me, I hand him
> over as myself. (18) And if he has done unjustly to you
> or owes you, put it on my account; (19) I, Paul, have
> written this with my hand, I will repay; in order that I
> may not say to you what also you yourself owe me. (20)
> Indeed, brother, I may profit by you in the lord; refresh
> my inmost being in Christ.

In this chapter, I will reserve judgment as to whether Paul's request to Philemon to receive Onesimus back "not as a slave but more than a slave, a beloved brother, especially to me, how much more rather to you also in the flesh and in the lord" (v. 16) was an appeal for manumission. Marianne Meye Thompson's insistence that Pauline anthropology does not allow a dualism between body ("in the flesh") and spirit ("in the lord") is worth considering: "To imagine that unity in Christ does not assume tangible shape in the church, in relationships among people, and in the church's witness to and work in the world simply sells out the reconciling gospel of Jesus Christ."[70] In the case of a "son" and "brother" whom Paul felt so strongly about, it would be strange if he didn't hope that Philemon would release Onesimus from slavery. Paul's admonition that Philemon should accept Onesimus back "as himself" (v. 17) supports this view; Paul, although captive in prison, had the status of a freeborn man—Onesimus should thus be freed. If this is what Paul was getting at, Onesimus would undoubtedly have hoped for his freedom even more than Paul. That said, admonitions to treat slaves kindly were not unusual in antiquity; nor were assertions of the "brotherhood" of slave and free.[71] These lofty ideals did

---

69. Escott, *Slavery Remembered*, 22–27.

70. Thompson, *Colossians and Philemon*, 247.

71. See Longenecker, *Philemon*, 181.

nothing to disrupt the slave system. This observation applies to the early church; as Mitzi Smith observes, "terms of endearment did not mitigate the slave-master relationship (see Eph. 5:21—6:9; Col. 3:1—4:1; 1 Tim. 6:1, 2; Titus 2:1–10; 1 Pet. 2:18–37)."[72] Obviously, since slaves were part of early Christian congregations, many believers accepted enslaved brothers and sisters as part of the body of Christ (Gal 3:28; 1 Cor 12:13; Col 3:11; Eph 6:8)—and continued to do so for many centuries.

Allen Dwight Callahan has argued that Paul's admonition to Philemon to welcome Onesimus back as "not as a slave but more than a slave, a beloved brother, . . . in the flesh and in the lord" (v. 16) should be interpreted not as a plea on behalf of an errant slave, but as an attempt to mend a rift between two estranged brothers, i.e., for Callahan, the "slavery" of Onesimus was metaphorical, but his "brotherhood" with Philemon was literal.[73] Callahan's hypothesis has not received much scholarly acceptance, but it does remind us that blood relationships within slaveholding households were complex. Due to the sexual access of slaveholders to slaves, a household could comprise free and enslaved relatives—Onesimus could have been the half-brother of Philemon, or even his son by an enslaved mother. In either case, the relationship would have been unacknowledged publicly, even if his real paternity were suspected. If Philemon was a freedman, he might well have had relatives still in slavery, whom he might or might not be willing, or able, to redeem. Likewise, Onesimus might have had relatives who were freedmen/women. He would almost certainly know other slaves who were the offspring of free slaveholders and enslaved women. Onesimus, then, would have been well aware of the porosity of the slave-freed-free continuum. The American abolitionist George Bourne was both right and wrong when he sarcastically observed with reference to Philemon: "Some conjecture from the expression, 'in the flesh,' used in the same 16th verse, that Onesimus was a natural brother of Philemon, in which case there is no probability that the former was a slave, as the practice of

---

72. Smith, "Philemon," 607.

73. Callahan, *Embassy of Onesimus*, 44–54.

enslaving such near relations was not common among the ancient heathen as it is now among modern Christians."[74] Both ancient and antebellum households included half-siblings on both sides of the slave/free divide; in both cases, slaveholders had no scruples about enslaving and selling their slave-born relations.

Many commentators have assumed that the reference in vv. 18–19 to a possible injustice or debt owed by Onesimus to Philemon that Paul was willing to repay pertains to theft. A common stereotype about slaves, ancient and American, is their proneness to thievery.[75] This stereotype is clearly articulated elsewhere in the NT: "Tell slaves to be submissive to their masters and to give satisfaction in every respect; they are not to answer back, not to pilfer, but to show complete and perfect fidelity, so that in everything they may be an ornament to the doctrine of God our Saviour" (Titus 2:9–10). As Joshel observes, the attribution of theft and other forms of criminality to slaves reflects the perspective of slaveholders: "The question, then, is to separate behavior and interpretation. The stereotypes of slaves and slaveholders' complaints represent slave owners' interpretation of slave behavior, and we are not bound to accept that understanding and explanation. . . . When Columella accuses slaves of stealing grain, he criminalizes slaves' appropriation of what their labor produced—or, in some cases, food for survival."[76] Joshel cites the example of Frederick Douglass, who developed a sophisticated rationale for his resort to theft:

> After much reflection I reasoned myself into the conviction that there was no other way to do, and that after all there was no wrong in it. Considering that my labor and person were the property of Master Thomas and that I was deprived of the necessaries of life—necessaries obtained by my own labor—it was easy to deduce the right to supply myself with what was my own. It was simply appropriating what was my own to the use of my master,

74. Quoted in Callahan, *Embassy of Onesimus*, 50.

75. Joshel, *Slavery in the Roman World*, 154–58, 178; Glancy, *Slavery in Early Christianity*, 134; Feldstein, *Once a Slave*, 172–75.

76. Joshel, *Slavery in the Roman World*, 156.

since the health and strength derived from such food were exerted in his service.[77]

In addition, as Feldstein notes, slaves were often falsely accused of criminality: "It was not unusual for a slave to be beaten to death or close to death for an unjust accusation of theft."[78] In the case of Onesimus, the charge is vague and hypothetical: "And if he has done unjustly to you or owes you, put it on my account" (v. 18). As with the assertion of Onesimus' previous "uselessness," the supposition of his pre-conversion dishonesty may simply be an expression of the stereotype of servile criminality. Alternatively, if, as suggested earlier, Onesimus was sent to Paul by Philemon to assist him during his incarceration, he would have been provided with some financial resources for his own support that Philemon might have wanted to recoup. Another possibility is that if, in fact, Onesimus was saving to buy his own manumission, Paul was offering to pay the difference between Onesimus's savings (*peculium*)[79] and the purchase price so that he could continue his service to the gospel as a freedman.

Paul's promise to repay any debt that Onesimus may have owed is pointedly described as written with his own hand (v. 19), an assurance found in several Pauline letters (1 Cor 16:21; Gal 6:11; cf. 2 Thess 3:17; Col 4:18). This indicates that the bulk of the letter was dictated to a scribe. If Onesimus was a literate slave, possibly he was the scribe who took down the letter.[80] A clear example of a scribe with a common servile name mentioned in a Pauline letter is Tertius ("third") (Rom 16:22): "I Tertius, the writer of this letter, greet you in the lord."[81] This admittedly speculative suggestion is supported by the fact that ancient scribes, like

77. Joshel, *Slavery in the Roman World*, 157–58, quoting Douglass, *Life and Times*, 104–5. See also Feldstein, *Once a Slave*, 175.

78. Feldstein, *Once a Slave*, 175.

79. On the peculium, see Joshel, *Slaves in the Roman World*, 128; Gamauf, "Slaves Doing Business," 334–35.

80. E.g., Elliott, *Family Empires*.

81. See Welborn, *An End to Enmity*, 235.

Tertius, were often slaves.[82] Onesimus' literacy would be an asset to a prisoner like Paul, dependant on others to relay messages to his supporters. If Onesimus was, in fact, a skilled amanuensis, the oft-remarked rhetorical finesse of the letter can be ascribed, in part, to him. The section ends with a third usage of the term *splagchna* (v. 20), translated above as "refresh my inmost being in Christ." As Osiek observes, this reference reminds Philemon of their common incorporation in Christ[83]—a christological incorporation that includes Onesimus.

### Conclusion and Final Greeting

(21) Having confidence in your obedience, I have written to you, knowing that concerning what I say you will do more. (22) Also, at the same time, prepare for me a guest room, for I hope that through your prayers I shall be restored to you. (23) My fellow captive Epaphras greets you in Christ Jesus, (24) as do Mark, Aristarchus, Demas, Luke, my co-workers. (25) The grace of Christ Jesus be with your spirit.

It is often noted that Epaphras (Paul's "fellow captive"), Mark, Aristarchus, Demas, and Luke (vv. 23–24) are also mentioned in Colossians (4:10, 12, 14). The greetings from five of Paul's associates implicitly support Paul's request regarding Onesimus. Any or all of them could have been slaves or freedmen at time of writing; the name Epaphras, particularly, had a "predominant association with slaves."[84] Michael Trainor goes so far as to suggest that the name of Epaphras, a slave or former slave, is mentioned first in Paul's list of greeters in order to add strength to Paul's appeal on behalf of Onesimus.[85]

---

82. Welborn, *An End to Enmity*, 235.

83. Osiek, *Philemon*, 141.

84. Trainor, *Epaphras*, 9.

85. Trainor, *Epaphras*, 9.

It's not certain that Paul's confidence that he would have the opportunity to visit Philemon's household was justified (v. 22). However, if as most commentators suggest, Onesimus was the messenger who delivered the letter to him, he would have been there when it was read. We will never know if Onesimus travelled back to Colossae on his own, or with other believing brothers and sisters, or exactly what happened when he arrived. Bruce Longenecker observes:

> Some have thought that Onesimus himself would have read the letter aloud to Philemon. This is unlikely. The letter makes a significant request (albeit largely unspecified) of an aggrieved slave master, encouraging him to make a beneficial decision regarding the fate of his slave, with significant rhetorical pressure being placed upon the master in the process; such a letter is unlikely to have been read to the master by the slave himself. That would have raised the stakes far too high, forcing the situation to become unnecessarily adversarial.[86]

Longenecker's surmise that he would "slink into the background while the letter was being read"[87] unnecessarily projects "slavish" behavior onto Onesimus. It is just as, or more, likely that Philemon would initially have read the letter himself, and perhaps consulted trusted members of the *ecclesia* (like his co-addressees Apphia and Archippus), before he, or someone else, read it aloud to the congregation. If he were unclear on Paul's intent, Onesimus would have been there to explain it to him, and to the *ecclesia* that met in his house, in the place of Paul himself (v. 17). The fact that such a brief, theologically undistinguished and rhetorically obscure document was preserved and ultimately made it into the Christian canon suggests that it—and the man who bore it—received a favorable response, whatever that response may have been.

---

86. Thompson and Longenecker, *Philippians and Philemon*, 162.
87. Thompson and Longenecker, *Philippians and Philemon*, 162.

# 3

# On Behalf of Onesimus

THE CORRESPONDENCE OF PLINY the Elder to Sabianus, interceding on behalf of an unnamed freedman for the forgiveness of his patron, has been both compared and contrasted with Paul's letter to Philemon:

> Your freedman, whom you lately mentioned to me with displeasure, has been with me, and threw himself at my feet with as much submission as he could have fallen at yours. He earnestly requested me with many tears, and even with all the eloquence of silent sorrow, to intercede for him; in short, he convinced me by his whole behaviour that he sincerely repents of his fault. I am persuaded he is thoroughly reformed, because he seems deeply sensible of his guilt. I know you are angry with him, and I know, too, it is not without reason; but clemency can never exert itself more laudably than when there is the most cause for resentment. You once had an affection for this man, and, I hope, will have again; meanwhile, let me only prevail with you to pardon him. If he should incur your displeasure hereafter, you will have so much the stronger plea in excuse for your anger as you shew yourself more merciful to him now. Concede something to his youth, to his tears, and to your own natural mildness of temper: do not make him uneasy any longer, and I will add, too, do not make yourself so; for a man of your kindness of heart cannot be angry without feeling great uneasiness. I am afraid, were I to join my entreaties with his, I should

seem rather to compel than request you to forgive him. Yet I will not scruple even to write mine with his; and in so much the stronger terms as I have very sharply and severely reproved him, positively threatening never to interpose again in his behalf. But though it was proper to say this to him, in order to make him more fearful of offending, I do not say so to you. I may perhaps, again have occasion to entreat you upon his account, and again obtain your forgiveness; supposing, I mean, his fault should be such as may become me to intercede for, and you to pardon. Farewell. (*Ep.* 9.21)

We know from Pliny's follow-up that his intercession on behalf of the freedman was effective:

I greatly approve of your having, in compliance with my letter, received again into your favour and family a discarded freedman, whom you once admitted into a share of your affection. This will afford you, I doubt not, great satisfaction. It certainly has me, both as a proof that your passion can be controlled, and as an instance of your paying so much regard to me as either to yield to my authority or to comply with my request. Let me, therefore, at once both praise and thank you. At the same time I must advise you to be disposed for the future to pardon the faults of your people, though there should be none to intercede in their behalf. Farewell. (*Ep.* 9.24)[1]

1. Pliny the Younger, *Letters*, trans. William Melmoth. Another ancient reference sometimes mentioned as a comparison with Philemon is Seneca's story of Augustus' attempt to intervene in the cruel murder of a slave (Seneca, *On Anger* 3.40): "To reprove a man when he is angry is to add to his anger by being angry oneself. You should approach him in different ways and in a compliant fashion, unless perchance you be so great a personage that you can quash his anger, as the Emperor Augustus did when he was dining with Vedius Pollio. One of the slaves had broken a crystal goblet of his: Vedius ordered him to be led away to die, and that too in no common fashion: he ordered him to be thrown to feed the muraenae, some of which fish, of great size, he kept in a tank. Who would not think that he did this out of luxury? but it was out of cruelty. The boy slipped through the hands of those who tried to seize him, and flung himself at Caesar's feet in order to beg for nothing more than that he might die in some different way, and not be eaten. Caesar was shocked at this novel form of cruelty, and ordered him to be let go, and, in his place, all the

Clearly, there are many differences between Paul's letter and Pliny's. The person for whom Pliny intercedes is a freedman (*libertus*), not a slave. Unlike Onesimus, the freedman is not named. Pliny describes the distress and penitence of the freedman in great detail, whereas Paul says nothing about Onesimus' demeanor. Pliny mentions his sharp rebuke of the freedman and asks Sabianus on his behalf for forgiveness of the suppliant's offence; Paul does not reproach Onesimus' behavior or ask for forgiveness. Pliny's correspondence includes a follow-up letter (*Ep.* 9.24), that indicates that Sabianus took his advice and pardoned the freedman. In contrast to Pliny's letter, which makes it crystal clear that he wanted Sabianus to forgive the freedman, it is notoriously difficult to gauge what Paul is requesting on behalf of (*peri*) Onesimus (Phlm 10); as Barclay put it "the letter is skilfully written to constrain Philemon to accept Paul's request, and yet, at the same time, it is extremely unclear what precisely Paul is requesting!"[2] However, Pliny's letter does resemble Paul's in that the apostle compliments Philemon on his good character (vv. 4–7), assumes a position of authority relative to him (v. 8), and diplomatically leaves the satisfactory response to the matter up to him (v. 14). Unlike Pliny's letter, there is no direct evidence as to how Paul's letter was received by Philemon and the *ecclesia* to which he belonged (Phlm 2), but as noted earlier, the very fact that it was preserved and circulated suggests that it was received and acted upon favorably.[3]

---

crystal ware which he saw before him to be broken, and the tank to be filled up" (trans. Aubrey Stewart). For references to similar intercessions on behalf of errant slaves, see Harrill, *Slaves in the New Testament*, 8–9; and Frilingos, "'For My Child, Onesimus,'" 91 n. 1 (https://en.wikisource.org/wiki/Of_Anger/Book_III#XL.). Tacitus recounts an incident where the Roman populace rallied to urge clemency in the case of the murder by his slave of the city prefect Pedanius Secundus, a crime that by tradition required the execution of all the slaves in his household; unfortunately for the slaves, the advocates of execution prevailed (Tacitus, *Annals* 14.42–45).

2. Barclay, "Paul, Philemon and the Dilemma of Christian Slave-Ownership," 170–71.

3. For evidence of lost or discarded Pauline letters, see 1 Cor 5:9; 2 Cor 2:4; 7:8–9; Col 4:15; Eph 3:3–4.

An under-appreciated similarity between Pliny's letter and Paul's is that both were written at the behest of a suppliant. According to Pliny, the freedman of Sabianus shed many tears, and made many entreaties (*flevit multum, multum rogavit*) for his mediation. Paul appeals to Philemon "on behalf of" (*peri*) his newly birthed "child," Onesimus (v. 10). Although the preposition *peri* with the genitive is often translated simply as "for" or "concerning," with "certain verbs and nouns such as 'ask,' 'pray,' 'prayer,' etc., περί introduces the pers[on] or thing in whose interest the petition is made. Thus it takes the place of 'ὑπέρ" (BDAG, 797). Such verbs include *parakaleō*, the verb that precedes the preposition in Paul's request: "I appeal to you (*parakalō se*), *on behalf of* my child (*peri tou emou teknou*), Onesimos, whom I begot/birthed while in chains."[4] That is, although Paul frames his request in terms of his own wish to keep Onesimus with him ("I wanted to keep him with me, so that he might be of service to me in your place during my imprisonment for the gospel," v. 13), the phraseology suggests that the ultimate source of the appeal is Onesimus, whom Paul speaks "on behalf of," and who already has expressed his will to become part of the believing community (v. 10). Far from being simply a transaction between two free men, the slave Onesimus has told Paul that he would prefer to remain with him in the service (*diakonē̄*) of the gospel; Paul conveys Onesimus' wishes as the same as his own: "I am sending him, that is, my own heart, back to you. I wanted to keep him with me" (vv. 12–13). The reference to Onesimus' serving Paul on Philemon's behalf (*hyper sou moi diakonē̄*) may rest on a conventional understanding of the slave as extension of the master,[5] but more than this, Paul implies that Onesimus has taken the place of Philemon in his ministry. The slave has joined the master in the "inner being" (*splanchna*) of the apostle and in the service of the gospel. Onesimus, sent to Paul as a

4. Other translations that render *peri* in Phlm 10 as "on behalf of" include the EHV, GNT, ISV, MEV, NABRE, TPT, and VOICE. For the translation of *egenēsan* ("begot/gave birth to"), see chap. 4.

5. Or even as a sexual outlet for the master and other free members of the household; Marchal, "Usefulness of an Onesimus," 749–70.

slave as an instrument of Philemon, returns to Philemon as a child of Paul and beloved brother in the *ecclesia*.

Whether Philemon actually sent Onesimus back to Paul simply as a loan, as a gift, or as a freedman (v. 16) is impossible to adjudicate. A slaveholder's perspective on the letter is illustrated by the slave-owning preacher Charles Colcock Jones, who self-servingly interpreted Philemon as a letter of intercession written by Paul on behalf of an enslaved brother. For Jones (who accepted the traditional "runaway slave" hypothesis), Paul was not requesting manumission, but simply asking that Onesimus be accepted by Philemon as a Christian slave: "And what do we see the same Apostle do? He restores the 'unprofitable' Onesimus to Philemon his master, though he had escaped from him to a great distance. Thus putting in to practice his own views and precepts. He calls the converted slave 'a brother beloved,' now to be specially regarded by Philemon, not only as a servant 'in the flesh' but as a Christian servant 'in the Lord.'"[6] Jones's paraphrase assumes that Paul's request that Philemon receive Onesimus "not as a slave but more than a slave, a beloved brother" (v. 16) is an assertion that a slave can be a believing "brother" and still remain a slave, a position that Christian slaveholders held firmly for many centuries, and which did not necessarily result in any amelioration of the treatment of enslaved believers. The question whether Onesimus' new spiritual status "in the flesh and in the Lord" (v. 16) would have had a positive impact on his life in Philemon's household is an open one.

From Onesimus' perspective, being transferred to the service of Paul in Ephesus (v. 13) could be advantageous. As the agent of the imprisoned Paul, he would enjoy relative freedom of movement in conveying messages and material support between the apostle and the local *ecclesia*. He might be entrusted to travel further afield to churches in the region, as imagined in Col 4:9. He might eventually be able to persuade the members of the community in Ephesus to buy him out of slavery,[7] if Philemon was

6. Jones, *Religious Instruction of Negroes*, 200.

7. For references to ecclesial manumission of Christian slaves, see Herm. Sim. 1.8; Herm. Mand. 8.10; Ignatius, *Pol.* 4.3; *Apostolic Constitutions* 4.9.2;

not willing to manumit him at Paul's behest. To the extent that Onesimus' implicit request to return to Paul as a partner in the service of the gospel was granted by Philemon, he would have had the hope of changing his lot in life for the better.

## Letters from Slaves

Several letters originating from nineteenth-century American slaves enable suggestive, albeit rough, comparisons with Philemon. These are letters to former masters dictated to, and mediated by, slaveholders. They are letters requesting important favors. In view of their great intrinsic interest, and their possible utility in understanding the Philemon letter, I quote them in full below.

In 1857, Vilet Lester appealed to her former owner, "Miss Patsy," in a letter transcribed by her then-owner, James Lester:

Georgia Bullock Co August 29th 1857

My Loving Miss Patsy

I hav long bin wishing to imbrace this presant and pleasant opertunity of unfolding my Seans and fealings Since I was constrained to leav my Long Loved home and friends which I cannot never gave my Self the Least promis of returning to. I am well and this is Injoying good hlth and has ever Since I Left Randolph. whend I left Randolf I went to Rockingham and Stad there five weaks and then I left there and went to Richmon virgina to be Sold and I Stade there three days and was bought by a man by the name of Groover and braught to Georgia and he kept me about Nine months and he being a trader Sold me to a man by the name of Rimes and he Sold me to a man by the name of Lester and he has owned me four years and Says that he will keep me til death Siperates us without Some of my old north Caroliner friends wants to buy me again. my Dear Mistress I cannot tell my fealings nor how bad I wish to See you and old Boss and

---

2.62.4; cf. 5.1–2; Patrick, *Letter to Coroticus* 14. See also Harrill, *Manumission of Slaves*, 178–82.

Mss Rahol and Mother. I do not [k]now which I want to
See the worst Miss Rahol or mother I have thaugh[t] that
I wanted to See mother but never befour did I [k]no[w]
what it was to want to See a parent and could not. I wish
you to gave my love to old Boss Miss Rahol and bailum
and gave my manafold love to mother brothers and sister
and pleas to tell them to Right to me So I may here from
them if I cannot See them and also I wish you to right
to me and Right me all the nuse. I do want to [k]now
whether old Boss is Still Living or now and all the rest of
them and I want to [k]now whether balium is maried or
no. I wish to [k]now what has Ever become of my Presus
little girl. I left her in goldsborough with Mr. Walker and
I have not herd from her Since and Walker Said that he
was going to Carry her to Rockingham and gave her to
his Sister and I want to [k]no[w] whether he did or no as
I do wish to See her very mutch and Boss Says he wishes
to [k]now whether he will Sell her or now and the least
that can buy her and that he wishes a answer as Soon as
he can get one as I wis him to buy her an my Boss being
a man of Reason and fealing wishes to grant my trubled
breast that mutch gratification and wishes to [k]now
whether he will Sell her now. So I must come to a close
by Escribing my Self you long loved and well wishing
play mate as a Servant until death.

Vilet Lester of Georgia
to Miss Patsey Padison of North Caroliner

My Bosses Name is James B Lester and if you Should think
a nuff of me to right me which I do beg the faver of you
as a Sevant direct your letter to Millray Bullock County
Georgia. Pleas to right me So fare you well in love.[8]

A second letter is briefer, and originated from an enslaved
man known only as "Charles" (then in Alabama), written to his
former owner William Greenaway (in Nottaway County, Virginia,
1825) also requesting family information:

8. Bullock County, Georgia. Vilet Lester to Patsey Patterson, August 29,
1857. https://library.duke.edu/specialcollections/scriptorium/lester/lester.html.

Tho I may ere this be obliterated from your memory, you and family and connexions are yet remembered by me with grateful feelings. It has been a long time since I heard from you all, my brother Jacob, if he is yet alive perhaps may suppose that I am no more but thanks be to all superintending power I am yet numbered among the living and in enjoyment of health and strength superior to most of my age. I belong to Mr. David Callahan to whom I have belonged for 25 years or upwards—it would be extremely consoling to me to hear from my Brother, and his welfare would exhilerate [sic] and strengthen me in my declining years. I have heard that you design moving to the state of Alabama. If you so will pass by where I live as I live in a mile of the road you must travel if you come thro Campbell. Should you come through this road if you will name me at Master Thomas Williams's he will contrive me word and I may yet have the satisfaction of seeing you and my Brother Jacob who I suppose will go with you—at any event will you my dear Master write to me. Please inform by Brother of the receipt of this and convey him with my best wishes for his health and happiness and accept dear Master for yourself and your family the unfeigned affection of an old family servant. Charles, formerly Joseph Greenhill.[9]

A third letter from an enslaved woman named Delia, dated October 1954, makes a similar request. In this case, the letter was likely written by the woman herself to her owner, Rice Ballard, a slave-trader, although she mentions the cooperation of Ballard's wife ("Mist Louiser") in the matter. She was writing from the Ballard family home in Louisville, KY to her master, who was at his plantation in Vicksburg, TN:[10]

Master I take this liberty to ask you Pleas to bye Henry and let him com home and live with me. Pleas overlook my not asking you to bye him when you was here but

9. Letter from Charles Barrow, formerly Joseph Greenhill, to William Greenhill, July 31, 1825. Mss1BB6108a221, Virginia Historical Society, Richmond. Quoted in Williams, *Help Me to Find My People*, 104.

10. See Williams, *Help Me to Find My People*, 67.

I thought you were angry with him because he did not agree to come to you when you offered to bye him. Master, you no [know] the nature of a man when he is got a family it is to make all he can for them henry only objection of living with you was because he could not make anything in a private house. When he found out he was forced to leave me it was like taking his life and I suppose he be com despat [desperate] and thought if he could make his escape. Master please over look his fault and bye my housband if you pleas, you [k]no[w] how hard it is to leave your family when you no there [they] are all well provided I hope you will think for a moment how hard it is my housband is take away from me I never expect to see him agen in this world no master please buy him. I have done all I can if you don't bye him please get some body to bye him that will let him come and see me Miss Louiser has promist me that you would ask you to bye him. Your resectly [respectfully] humble servant Delia.[11]

In another letter, written on behalf of an enslaved man named Nathan, Garret Duncan wrote to the lawyer Orlando Brown, begging him to sell Nathan's wife to someone in the vicinity of Louisville so that he could be nearer to her: "He says to avoid the necessity of changing about as hired servants have to do he would look out for a good master and prevail on some friends to buy his wife if you are willing to sell her."[12]

Despite the vast historical and cultural gulf between Philemon and the letters of Vilet, Charles, Delia, and Nathan, some similarities stand out. All are letters asking for an important boon for an enslaved person from a master written with the assistance of a member of the "master class": Paul (Onesimus), James Lester (Vilet), David Callahan (Charles), Louisa Ballard (Delia), Orlando Brown (Nathan). Vilet's letter was clearly dictated to her current "Boss," whom she compliments as "a man of Reason and fealing." It is unclear whether Charles himself or someone else wrote his

11. Letter from Delia, Louisville, KY, October 22, 1854, Rice C. Ballard Papers, USC. Transcribed Williams, *Help Me to Find My People*, 66–69

12. Blassingame, *Slave Testimony*, 28.

letter to William Greenaway, but he would have been dependent on "Master Thomas Williams" to agree with his plan, and, perhaps had his assistance in writing the letter. Delia states that she had enlisted Louisa Ballard's support for her request. Garnett Duncan served as Nathan's agent. In all these cases, the letters concerned family matters: Vilet wanted information about her daughter so that her current owner could buy her and reunite them; Charles was anxious to see a brother he hadn't seen in at least twenty-five years; Delia wanted Rice Ballard to buy her enslaved husband Henry, an ex-fugitive, so they could live together; similarly, Nathan wanted his wife to be purchased by someone in the same city so he could visit her. Although, compared with Philemon, the voices of the enslaved senders come through loud and clear—they wanted to be reunited with their loved ones (or at least receive some news of them)—"these people relied on their owners and former owners to get their messages through."[13] In other words, the "master class" collaborators in the writing of these letters were acting "on behalf of" enslaved persons whose fervent wishes they were helping to relay. The assistance afforded the enslaved writers was in keeping with the paternalistic self-image of slaveholders, both in antiquity and in antebellum America, who regarded themselves (contrary to ample evidence in the slave narratives) as judicious guardians of their slaves' health and welfare, meting out rewards and punishments fairly and efficiently for the smooth and profitable functioning of their property.[14] Philemon would have shared this idealized perception of himself as a "good" master who managed his household in a reasonable and just way; although the enslaved members of his *oikos* might well have thought differently, they would know that he would respond favorably to being addressed as such.

The letters of Vilet and Charles, particularly, are similar to Philemon in that both couch their requests in effusive (and in Vilet's case, lengthy) expressions of regard for "Master": "I hav long bin wishing to imbrace this presant and pleasant opertunity of unfolding my Seans and fealings Since I was constrained to

13. Williams, *Help Me to Find My People*, 126.
14. Del Lago and Katsari, "Ideal Models of Slave Management."

leav my Long Loved home. . . . Escribing my Self you long loved and well wishing play mate as a Servant until death " (Vilet); "Tho I may ere this be obliterated from your memory, you and family and connexions are yet remembered by me with grateful feelings. . . . [A]ccept dear Master for yourself and your family the unfeigned affection of an old family servant" (Charles); Delia signs off deferentially as a "humbly respectful servant." Garnett Duncan reports that Nathan's wife did not "wish or ever to expect to find a better master than you have been."[15] Similarly, the letter to Philemon: "I give thanks to my God always making mention of you in my prayers, hearing of the love and faith you have for Christ Jesus and toward all the holy ones . . . . For they have much joy and encouragement from your love, because the inward parts of the holy ones are refreshed through you, brother" (vv. 4–5, 7). Perhaps like these slaves, Onesimus, through Paul, "carefully straddled the line between deference and assertiveness, . . . keenly aware of the delicate balance they had to strike in their communications with their former owners. They acknowledged their subordinate positions while they appealed to old loyalties, even perhaps old debts."[16] Similarly, the Philemon letter is both obsequious ("apart from your judgment I do not wish to do anything," v. 14) and assertive ("having much boldness to command you to what is necessary, rather through love I request," vv. 8–9), and invokes old loyalties and debts: "Since you are in partnership with me, I hand him over as myself. And if he has done unjustly to you or owes you, put it on my account; I, Paul, have written this with my hand, I will repay; in order that I may not say to you what also you yourself owe me" (vv. 17–19).

Despite the involvement of "masters" in the writing process, we can read between the lines of the letters of the nineteenth-century slaves to discern the hidden transcripts of their real feelings. All of them were, as Delia put it, "despat" (desperate) to reunite with family members forcibly separated from them by sale, or, in the case of Delia's husband Henry, flight and recapture. Regardless

15. Blassingame, *Slave Testimony*, 29.
16. Del Lago and Katsari, "Ideal Models of Slave Management," 130.

of their rhetorical expressions of appreciation for "master," they and their relatives had suffered being consigned to the slave market by them (and likely many other abuses besides); even James Lester, the "man of Reason and fealing" was willing to sell Vilet (although apparently not to emancipate her) if "Some of my old north Caroliner friends wants to buy me again." Like other slaveholders of the time, the men addressed by these enslaved people were so oblivious to the inner lives ("soul value") of their "property" that they believed that someone like Vilet would want to see Miss Patsy and Boss even more than she yearned to see her mother—and, above all, her precious daughter; or that Charles wanted to see his former master (who had sold him away) as much as he longed to visit with his brother Jacob.[17] Despite the slaves' stated confidence in the good will of the slaveholders, like Philemon, they held all the cards: they could choose to grant these requests, or ignore them. Rather than granting Delia's request, Ballard could have punished her for her presumption. Paul's assurance of Philemon's "obedience" (v. 21) to his petition "on behalf of Onesimus" was purely hypothetical. All of them were part of a system where rewards and punishments upheld the dominance of masters over their households:

> [I]n both cases, the system of punishment and rewards also made clear in an equally tangible way that the slaves' improvement of their own condition could occur only within the set boundaries of the master-slave relationship. In other words, such an improvement could occur only through the slaves' acknowledgment of their masters' authority and their acceptance of their absolute dependence on his goodwill for their well-being. As a consequence, in both the Roman world and the ante-bellum American South, the ideal model of slave management came to be based on a system of punishment and reward that was not only strongly ideologically charged, but that was specifically meant to reinforce the hierarchy and structure of power that had originated from the formation of the slave society.[18]

17. Cf. Del Lago and Katsari, "Ideal Models of Slave Management," 140.
18. Dal Lago and Katsari, "Ideal Models of Slave Management," 199.

The letters of the nineteenth-century suppliants, like Philemon, were preserved by the slaveholders, but we don't know how, or if, they answered them.

The similarities between the rhetorical strategies used by Vilet, Charles, and Delia in addressing their "masters," on the one hand, and Paul to Philemon, on the other, may be purely an artefact of effective writing; by no means do they prove that Onesimus had a hand in the crafting of the letter. Maximally, Onesimus may have been the scribe who took down Paul's words up to v. 19 ("I, Paul, have written this with my own hand"), and whose wishes for himself coincided with those of his spiritual parent (v. 10). Minimally, he would have been a passive pawn in a transaction between two "masters"—although Paul, confined to a Roman prison for an indefinite period pending trial, would have had less personal freedom of movement than Onesimus at the time of writing (see chapter 4). But, as suggested in the last chapter, it is not unlikely that Onesimus was aware of Paul's wishes for him and had some role in the formulation of the letter written on his behalf.

## Letter Writing and Slave Agency

The letters quoted above illustrate that despite the state of "social death" in which they functioned, enslaved persons could use letters (among other tactics), with the assistance of sympathetic "masters," to convey their ardent wishes in terms designed to stroke slaveholders' egos and thereby gain their cooperation. As Sharoney Green observes of another letter written by the freedwoman Avenia White to Delia's master Rice Ballard, letter-writing allows for performance.[19] In addition to being a slave trader, Ballard trafficked in "fancy girls"—light-skinned enslaved women used as prostitutes and concubines; the women who figured in this correspondence likely had been among them. In Cincinatti in 1838 (probably with the assistance of her landlady, Mrs. Bruster), White dictated two letters to Ballard asking for financial assistance

19. Green, "Mr. Ballard," 30.

for herself, another freedwoman called Susan, and their children. Green summarizes the import of the two letters:

> "Mr Ballard, Sir, I write you a few lines" began Avenia, who also reported that she and Susan and the children were in good health but "somewhat depressed in spirits." It appears Bruster's boarding house was not close to "business." The kind of business to which she was referring is unclear, but it was likely something that could be found on the riverfront. Avenia yearned to be near the Ohio even as the region was experiencing a drought, which reduced the river's waterborne traffic. This bottleneck hurt commerce. The economic slowdown made local business owners reluctant to hire additional workers. With job prospects dim, Avenia asked Ballard for financial assistance so she and Susan could continue paying their rent and "purchase little articles toward housekeeping." . . . Their earnings, however, were not enough. They needed beds, she said. They also needed funds to buy wood for fuel as the night air was growing cooler. By now, their funds were so limited they had to borrow eight dollars from Mrs. Bruster, who was sending a hello. Avenia herself sent "love." She ended the letter with this postscript: "PS Harvey has been very sick. He is now recovering."
>
> Ballard did not reply to Avenia's letter. She decided to try again. On October 25, 1838, another letter was written. In this one, she stated, "I am compelled to write you again." She told Ballard that the river was still low and affecting business, which was having an impact on her and Susan's ability to find regular work. She was taking in sewing and laundry, and Susan was "compelled to go to service by the week," probably as a domestic worker.[20]

According to Green, the "performance" aspects of Avenia's letters consisted in their business-like tone, and, particularly, the double-edged use of conventional terminology like "humble servant" and "your most obedient servant."[21] She continues:

20. Green, "Mr. Ballard," 26–27.
21. Green, "Mr. Ballard," 30.

Avenia's use of the phrase "humble servant" points to more. The word "servant" seems to have been her unconscious attempt to win Ballard's favor. She did this, ironically, using a word that conjures imagery of her former status as a slave. Rest assured, she needed to do this. She needed him, but she had to state her need in a way that massaged his ego and safeguarded his racial dominance while simultaneously engaging his thirst for enterprise. In employing this phrase, Avenia was pushing several buttons in Ballard.[22]

As his former slave, "fancy girl," and likely mother of his children, Avenia knew which buttons to push by addressing Ballard with discreet, yet pointed, assertions of his responsibilities to his former slaves and their children. Ballard did, eventually, send money, although only after the intervention of a local city councillor and merchant whose name dropped into subsequent correspondence seems to have finally moved him: "Perhaps moved by her pleas or ashamed of how [councillor] Fletcher might regard his apparent neglect, Ballard sent money,"[23] which Avenia followed up with a thank you letter.[24]

22. Green, "Mr. Ballard," 30.

23. Green, "Mr. Ballard," 27.

24. Letters from former slaves no longer dependant on their former masters are drastically different in tone from those cited above. A famous example is Frederick Douglass's literary "Letter to My Old Master," which catalogues Thomas Auld's crimes against Douglass and his family, lists the great abolitionist's many successes since his flight, and assures Auld that he will be used as a weapon in the anti-slavery cause (https://allthatsinteresting.com/former-slave-letters/2). Another letter (possibly a forgery), by "Jourdan Anderson," was allegedly written in 1865 in response to an invitation from his former owner to return to his farm and work for wages. The author responded that he would rather "starve and die" than expose his daughters to the kind of abuse that young women had suffered due to the "conduct of their young masters," and pointedly asked whether any schools for "colored children" had been opened in his neighborhood, as his priority was the education of his family (https://www.neatorama.com/2012/01/30/letter-from-an-ex-slave-to-his-for-mer-master/). An undoubtedly genuine letter from Spotswood Rice, who had deserted Katherine Diggs's plantation in Missouri to join the Union army in 1864, is undisguisedly angry and threatening: "I want you to understand kittey diggs that where ever you and I meets we are enmays to each orthere I offered

Onesimus, like Avenia, knew "master" in a way that Paul did not. Did Onesimus help Paul to frame his letter in a way that would appeal to Philemon's preferences, moods, weaknesses, hypocrisies, and sensitivities? These might include the slaveholder's pride in his status within the *ecclesia*, his reputation for beneficence among fellow-believers, his authority over his dependants as paterfamilias, his judicious household management, his sense of prestige as one in *koinōnia* with the Pauline mission, his concern for the welfare of imprisoned believers (and perhaps his fear of becoming one of them), his dread of censure by his community, his kindness or cruelty to the slaves in his household. These matters will be pursued further in the Afterword.

---

once to pay you forty dollers for my own Child but I am glad now that you did not accept it Just hold on now as long as you can and the worse it will be for you never in you life befor I came down hear did you give Children any thing not eny thing whatever not even a dollers worth of expencs now you call my children your pro[per]ty not so with me my Children is my own and I expect to get them and when I get ready to come after mary I will have bout a powrer and autherity to bring hear away and to exacute vengencens on them that holds my Child" (https://www.neatorama.com/2012/03/01/letter-from-an-ex-slave-to-his-former-master-im-coming-to-get-you/). For further slave letters, see Blassingame, *Slave Testimony*; Work Projects Administration, *Voices from the Past*; Starobin, *Blacks in Bondage*.

# 4

# Borne in Chains

APART FROM SPECIFIC STUDIES of Paul as a Roman prisoner,[1] surprisingly few commentators make much of the prison setting of
the letter to Philemon. This chapter will focus specifically on the
references in the letter to Paul's imprisonment in order to imaginatively reconstruct how the presence of someone like Onesimus
would have figured as Paul awaited trial, and how this relates to
Onesimus' status vis-à-vis the *ecclesia*—the church in Philemon's
household, and the local Ephesian community. Throughout, I pre-
suppose, as argued in chapter 2, that Onesimus was not a runaway
slave, but, a "body in motion,"[2] serving as an intermediary between Paul and the local assembly of believers, and between Paul,
Philemon, and "the church in his house."

The letter begins with Paul's self-designation as "prisoner" of
the messiah, Jesus (v. 1). The word translated as prisoner (*desmios*)
literally refers to fetters or chains. Taken on its own, the reference
could simply be to Paul's metaphorical or spiritual bondage for the
sake of Jesus, but in context, it is clear that it is a usage suggested
by his own, actual imprisonment. Carolyn Osiek suggests that from
the outset, Paul may have sought "for rhetorical effect to identify
himself in some way with the status of Onesimus, though calling
himself the 'slave of Christ' as in Rom 1:1 or Phil 1:1 would have

1. E.g., Wansink, *Chained in Christ*, 174–99; Cassidy, *Paul in Chains*,
68–84.

2. Charles, *Silencing of Slaves*, 66.

been more effective for that purpose."[3] Throughout this letter, Paul's language of imprisonment and enslavement alternates between the literal and the metaphorical: he is "in chains" of/for Jesus Christ (v. 9); Onesimus is his child delivered "in chains" (v. 10); Paul wants Onesimus to serve him in the bonds/chains of the gospel (v. 13); Epaphras is Paul's fellow-prisoner for the sake of (and belonging to) Christ Jesus (v. 23). A literally enslaved person would have understood what it was like to be literally "in chains" as Paul was; chains were used to restrain slaves in a variety of contexts,[4] both as a physical restraint and a symbol of subjection (Figure 2).

Figure 2: Roman collared slaves

The prison setting adds a special poignancy to Paul's reference to his "child" Onesimus, "begotten" (as many translations put it) "in chains" (v. 10).[5] The verb *egenōsan* would normally, with a male subject, mean "beget," but with a feminine subject, the usual translation would be "to give birth to" (BDAG 193). There are

3. Osiek, *Philippians and Philemon*, 133.

4. Joshel, *Slavery in the Roman World*, 68, 84, 87, 90, 119–20, 131, 176, 177.

5. Other translations use a phrase like "whose father I have become" (e.g., NRSV, NAB; the NIV has "who became my son").

many ancient references to female prisoners giving birth in prison: "Raising a child in prison appears to have been a somewhat rare practice, although there are numerous accounts of women giving birth while there. Births in prison resulted, at least in part, from an Egyptian law which the Greeks and Romans adopted. This law stipulated that a pregnant woman under sentence of death would be allowed to remain alive in prison until the child was born."[6] A famous case is the imprisoned martyr Felicitas, who, eight months pregnant, gave birth to a daughter in time for her to die along with her fellow Christians (*Passion* 15). Women also conceived children in prison, many due to rape.[7] Wansink is one of the few interpreters who translates *hon egennōsa en tois desmois* (v. 10) as having "given birth to him in chains,"[8] perhaps because of his awareness of the actual conditions of Roman imprisonment, although he does not state this explicitly. Paul's imagery seems most likely to be that of a mother giving birth to a child in incredibly adverse conditions (although the plight of actual women giving birth in prison would have been much worse). Wansink notes that the expression *ta ema splangchna* (v. 12), discussed above in chapter 2, has another relevant meaning: "it is also a synonym of the Greek word παῖς (child). Artemidorus is explicit in *Oneirocritica*: 'Children' (οἱ παῖδες), like the inward parts of the body, are also called σπλάγχνα (1.44)."[9] Onesimus is the *pais/ta ema splagchna* metaphorically birthed by Paul in prison (v. 10, 12).

Unlike Paul, who could at least hope for release in the foreseeable future (v. 22), Onesimus' captivity was life-long, with a faint hope of manumission at the whim of the slaveholder, Philemon—a "promise of freedom held out as a reward for good behavior, loyalty, and service."[10] If, as some interpreters think, Paul was discreetly hinting that Philemon should manumit Onesimus so that he could be "freed" to "serve" Paul in spreading

6. Wansink, *Chained in Christ*, 56.

7. Wansink, *Chained in Christ*, 56–57.

8. Wansink, *Chained in Christ*, 177. See also Knox, *Philemon*, 5–6.

9. Wansink, *Chained in Christ*, 177.

10. Wansink, *Chained in Christ*, 128.

the gospel, he would undoubtedly have preferred the prospect of metaphorical to real-life bondage. However, for a believing slave like Onesimus, the slave/bondage metaphor could amount to "double trouble," as Marianne Bjelland Kartzow puts it. For an enslaved believer, "Slavery was not merely a thought figure; it was everyday reality for millions of men and women, children and adults."[11] Similarly, Paul had first-hand knowledge of what it was to be a real, as well as a metaphorical, "prisoner of Christ Jesus" (Phlm 1). He no doubt preferred the latter.

Whether Paul was imprisoned in Ephesus (cf. 1 Cor 15:32; 2 Cor 1:8–10), as I have argued, or in Rome, as the traditional interpretation holds, the letter to Philemon was composed during the same imprisonment as the Philippian letter—Paul's other, authentic, "prison epistle."[12] Elsa Tamez has commented at length upon the prison setting of Philippians, so her commentary is very helpful in the interpretation of Philemon, as well.[13] Moreover, as Wansink has pointed out, there is a similarity between the roles of Onesimus in Philemon and Epaphroditus in Philippians (Phil 2:25; 4:18) that has been overlooked by most commentators.[14] The Onesimus/Epaphroditus parallel will be discussed later in this chapter.

As with Philippians, when he dictated the letter to Philemon, Paul would have been in military custody (*custodia militaris*), "watched over by soldiers and chained permanently to them."[15] Of the three forms of Roman incarceration—the other two were *carcer*, where prisoners were held in a pit underground (the *tullianum*) (cf. Acts 16:22–24; *Perpetua and Felicity* 3), and *custodia libera* (house arrest)[16]—military custody was of intermediate

---

11. Kartzow, *Slave Metaphor*, 4.

12. Wansink, *Chained in Christ*, 175.

13. Tamez, *Philippians*, 3–35. See also Batten, *Philemon*, 236.

14. Wansink, *Chained in Christ*, 175.

15. Tamez, *Philippians*, 17.

16. Acts 12:16, 30–31 represents Paul as living under house arrest in Rome, but Standhartinger argues that a Jewish artisan like Paul would not be granted this privilege, which was reserved for the Roman elite ("Aus der Welt," 142–43).

severity.[17] However, as Tamez asserts: "this doesn't mean that Paul didn't suffer while under military custody, . . . Paul had to depend on the character or temperament of the soldier or soldiers to whom he was chained."[18]

In the Roman world, imprisonment was not regarded primarily as punishment for a crime; rather, it was a period of confinement prior to trial. This doesn't mean that long-term incarceration didn't happen—time-limited sentences did not exist, and prisoners could be held for a very long time.[19] Obviously, long-term confinement under adverse conditions was punitive in and of itself and took a psychological toll on prisoners awaiting trial at an unspecified date and with an uncertain outcome. Like other prisoners, Paul would have suffered "beatings, chains, darkness and squalor. . . . [I]mprisonment might lead to death: either execution by the authorities or death resulting from disease, torture or the psychological trauma of imprisonment itself."[20] Tamez thinks it probable that Paul was sentenced to death at Ephesus, and set free for some reason (1 Cor 15:32; 2 Cor 1:8–10; cf. 2 Cor 11:23)—perhaps due to an amnesty.[21] Despite his assertions of faith and confidence (cf. Phil 1:21; Phlm 22), the loss of his freedom, the harsh conditions in prison, and anxiety over at the future would have weighed on his mind and body. Paul's advice to Philemon to prepare a guest room for him (v. 22) may be little more than bravado meant to reassure both himself and the letter's recipients. If, as tradition holds, Paul was imprisoned in Rome and not Ephesus, then he was not released, but executed in a dark, subterranean *tullianum*.[22] It is under these circumstances that Onesimus' role is best understood.

As argued in chapter 2, the best explanation of Onesimus' presence with Paul is that he was sent by Philemon—and perhaps

---

17. Wansink, *Chained in Christ*, 40.

18 Tamez, *Philippians*, 17–18.

19. Wansink, *Chained in Christ*, 30.

20. Wansink, *Chained in Christ*, 33.

21. Tamez, *Philippians*, 12–13. Perhaps he got off with a flogging (cf. 2 Cor 11:23–25; Acts 5:40).

22. Tamez, *Philippians*, 12.

by the house church he belonged to—in order to be of service to the prisoner. Like other prisoners, Paul was in a precarious and vulnerable position, and, like other prisoners, he would have been highly dependent on visitors—members of the local *ecclesia*, other missionaries, and the slave sent to minister to him— for material, emotional and spiritual support. Roman prisoners relied on friends and family for basic necessities like food and clothing, bribes for guards, and legal assistance.[23] Wansink notes that "comforting and aiding the imprisoned was a common practice among the ancients."[24]

> Epicurus mentioned the importance of friends who would help those who were in prison or in want, and numerous examples of such help have been preserved. When Agrippa was imprisoned, his friend, Silas and two of his freemen brought his favorite food and did whatever they could for him, even fashioning a bed for him out of some garments. Cleomenes had his own slaves and attendants with him. And although Musionius discourages Appollonius from visiting him in prison, Appollonius declared his willingness to do so (referring to the prison as Musonius's "lodgings"): "I would fain come unto you, to share (κοινοῆσαι) your conversation and your lodgings (στέγη), in the hope of being of some use to you."[25]

The NT contains several references to prison visitation (Matt 25:36, 39, 43; Heb 10:34; 13:3; 2 Tim 1:17; cf. Acts 12:5; Luke 4:16). The greetings at the end of Paul's two authentic prison epistles (Phlm 24; Phil 4:21–22) likely refer to believers who had visited the apostle. The fact that Onesimus had been sent for his aid and comfort would undoubtedly have evoked Paul's gratitude for Philemon's generosity, which at least partially explains the lengthy thanksgiving in vv. 4–7. The "saints" who had received "much joy and encouragement" from the love of Philemon, whose "inward parts" were refreshed by him, included Paul himself. But for all Paul's gratitude

---

23. Tamez, *Philippians*, 12; Nicklas, "Care for Prisoners," 50, 58, 61.

24. Wansink, *Chained in Christ*, 191.

25. Wansink, *Chained in Christ*, 191–92.

for Philemon's assistance from a distance, it was delivered not by Philemon himself, but by Onesimus ("not . . . a slave but more than a slave, a beloved brother," v. 16), the person who was actually serving Paul on his master's behalf (v. 13).

Tamez's interviews with contemporary political prisoners reveal how important visitors are to the incarcerated; these interviews also contain Christian prisoners' reflections on Paul's experience in Philippians.[26] One theme is the importance of visitors: "They broke the record for prison visits. Like Paul, they visited me frequently. Saturday was visitation for the men, and women came on Sunday. . . . I told visitors not to bring me anything but to bring me the money they would have spent. With the money they brought to the jail I would maintain my husband and children as much as I was able. . . . Small things had a great value."[27] Neila Serrano de Barragán observed that visitors in line waiting to see prisoners were treated like prisoners themselves: "It is like telling them: you are as guilty as the one inside; you are worthless too."[28] Paul, de Barragán imagined, would have "enjoyed the strength they [women members of the Philippian community] were giving him, but he had to have many moments of kneeling and crying and asking God, the Lord Jesus Christ, to give him strength."[29] As the priest Frei Betto wrote in a letter to his friend Maria Christina, "In prison, one always waits."[30] Against this backdrop, Tamez observes that "in Philippians, Paul does not hide his great happiness at receiving the economic help and general support from the community at Philippi by way of Epaphroditus . . . (Phil 2:30; 4:10–18). Paul took great comfort as well from the presence of Timothy (Phil 2:19–24)."[31] She further notes that "Paul's letter to Philemon mentions the companionship and collaboration of Mark, Aristarchus, Demas, and Luke, as well

26. Tamez, *Philippians*, 23–35.

27. Tamez, *Philippians*, 29.

28. Tamez, *Philippians*, 31.

29. Tamez, *Philippians*, 32.

30. Tamez, *Philippians*, 25.

31. Tamez, *Philippians*, 13.

as Timothy and Onesimus (Phlm 24)."[32] In contrast, the Deutero-
Pauline 2 Timothy imagined Paul as a prisoner in Rome (1:17),
abandoned by all of his colleagues except for Onesiphorus, whose
visits he praised: "May the Lord grant mercy to the household of
Onesiphorus, because he often refreshed me and was not ashamed
of my chain" (1:17; cf. 4:19).

Against this backdrop, Paul's deep appreciation of Onesimus—
his "inmost being," his child birthed in chains, his beloved brother—
reflects the apostle's gratitude for the services he received from an
enslaved visitor sent in order to attend to his daily needs, material
and emotional. Onesimus' receptiveness to Paul's teaching would in
and of itself been a comfort to the apostle. In addition, the services
he rendered as a prison visitor would have elicited Paul's gratitude.
Josephus (*Antiquities* 6.6) recounts the lavish promises made by
Herod Agrippa, imprisoned by Tiberius, to the slave Thaumastus,
who granted his request for a drink of water:

> It was also very hot weather, and they had but little wine
> to their meal, so that he was very thirsty; he was also
> in a sort of agony, and took this treatment of him hei-
> nously: as he therefore saw one of Caius's slaves, whose
> name was Thaumastus, carrying some water in a vessel,
> he desired that he would let him drink; so the servant
> gave him some water to drink, and he drank heartily,
> and said, "O thou boy! this service of thine to me will
> be for thy advantage; for if I once get clear of these my
> bonds, I will soon procure thee thy freedom of Caius
> who has not been wanting to minister to me now I am
> in bonds, in the same manner as when I was in my for-
> mer state and dignity."

Agrippa was as good as his word:

> Nor did he deceive him in what he promised him, but
> made him amends for what he had now done; for when
> afterward Agrippa was come to the kingdom, he took
> particular care of Thaumastus, and got him his liberty
> from Caius, and made him the steward over his own

32. Tamez, *Philippians*, 13.

estate; and when he died, he left him to Agrippa his son,
and to Bernice his daughter, to minister to them in the
same capacity. The man also grew old in that honorable
post, and therein died. But all this happened a good
while later.[33]

The social gulf between the tentmaker Paul and the slave
Onesimus was nowhere near the gap between the aristocratic
Agrippa and Thaumastus, but the inordinate appreciation of a
king for a past act of simple kindness from a slave rings true; a
small thing with great value. It is plausible that the many services
rendered to the Paul by Onesimus "in the bonds of the gospel"
(v. 13) would have provoked even more intense feelings of gratitude in the vulnerable apostle.

As the quotation from Bárragan above observes, visitors to
contemporary political prisoners, as Paul was likely classified,[34]
run the risk of suspicion themselves. Similarly, in antiquity, association with prisoners placed friends, family, and especially
visitors under suspicion.[35] Letters from prison were subject to
censorship, and transcribing or delivering a letter from a prisoner could put the person involved in peril.[36] The satirist Lucian
of Samosata (second century CE) famously described crowds of
widows and orphans waiting to visit the prisoner Proteus/Pereg-
rinus early in the morning (*Peregrinus* 12). Lucian also mentions
Christian "officials" (*hoi de en telei autōn*) who slept with the
prisoner after bribing the guards. Although Lucian's account is
unsympathetic and written a century after the letter to Philemon,
his account of Peregrinus' incarceration, and the lengths to which
his coreligionists went to improve his situation, gives a hint of
what Paul, and his protégé, experienced. Was Onesimus sent to
minister to Paul because, as a slave, he was considered innocuous
and expendable, like the widows and orphans of Lucian's account?
Unlike friends and associates who had the option to abandon a

33. Whiston, *Works of Josephus*.

34. See Cassidy, *Paul in Chains*, 55–67.

35. Standhartinger, "Aus der Welt," 157; see also Tamez, *Philippians*, 15.

36. Tamez, *Philippians*, 15.

prisoner in order to save themselves,[37] like the disloyal Phygelus and Hermogenes, among others, mentioned in 2 Tim 1:15 ("You are aware that all who are in Asia have turned away from me, including Phygelus and Hermogenes"), widows, orphans, and a slave like Onesimus might have been viewed as members of the *ecclesia* the least likely to be suspected of subversion. Perhaps this is why Onesimus was sent "on behalf of" the slaveholder, Philemon, rather than Philemon attending Paul himself.

As mentioned earlier, there is a parallel to be made between the role of Epaphroditus in Philippians (2:25; 4:18) and Onesimus in Philemon. It is clear that Epaphroditus was sent by the Philippian community with "gifts" for the imprisoned apostle (4:18), as their "messenger and minister" to his needs (2:25). Wansink observes: "Just as churches in Asia are remembered as having sent support to Peregrinus and Paul, just as the Philippians sent Epaphroditus to minister to the imprisoned apostle, so the possibility needs to be considered that Philemon sent Onesimus as a messenger or minister to Paul's need: Onesimus was with Paul because he had been sent there."[38] Because the name Epaphroditus ("lovely" or "charming") was very common among slaves,[39] it is often assumed that he was a freedman,[40] although considering the parallel with Onesimus, there is no reason to assume that he, too, was not a slave. As Ronald Charles notes, like Onesimus, Epaphroditus was "a body in motion and as a ministering body susceptible to be exchanged or sent back and forth, which corresponds to the position of a slave or former slave attached to a former owner or patron."[41] Unlike Onesimus, however, it is clear that Epaphroditus, whether slave or freedman, was a committed member of the Philippian community, who "came close to death for the work of Christ, risking his life to make up for those services that you could not give me" (Phil 2:30). Onesimus, whether he was a believer

---

37. See Cassidy, *Paul in Chains*, 48–51.

38. Wansink, *Chained in Christ*, 193.

39. See Nasrallah, *Archaeology and the Letters of Paul*, 125.

40. See, e.g., Charles, *Silencing of Slaves*, 77–81.

41. Charles, *Silencing of Slaves*, 78.

before or only after he met Paul, likely ran similar risks serving the apostle "in the bonds of the gospel" (Phlm 13).

Wansink discusses another salient parallel that may shed light on the role of Onesimus. Following John Knox (with due reservations about Knox's over-enthusiasm regarding ambiguous evidence),[42] he cites the role of the deacon Burrhus in the Ignatius' *Letter to the Ephesians*, written early in the second century:

> As to my *fellow-servant* [*syndoulos*] Burrhus, your *deacon* [*diakonos*] in regard to God and blessed in all things, *I beg that he may continue longer*, both for your honour and that of your bishop. And Crocus also, worthy both of God and you, whom I have received as the manifestation of your love, has in all things *refreshed* me, as the Father of our Lord Jesus Christ shall also refresh him; together with *Onesimus*, and Burrhus, and Euplus, and Fronto, by means of whom, I have, as to love, beheld all of you. May I always have joy of you, if indeed I be worthy of it. It is therefore befitting that you should in every way glorify Jesus Christ, who has glorified you, that by a unanimous obedience "you may be perfectly joined together in the same mind, and in the same judgment, and may all speak the same thing concerning the same thing," and that, being subject to the bishop and the presbytery, you may in all respects be sanctified. (*Eph.* 2.1–2)[43]

At time of writing (early second century), Ignatius, bishop of Antioch, was under arrest and being transported to Rome. Perhaps because of the similarity between his own position and the imprisoned Paul's, Ignatius deliberately echoed the letter to Philemon: Burrhus is referred to as a "fellow slave" (*syndoulos*), recalling Onesiumus the *doulos*; Paul wished that Onesimus could stay with him longer to "serve" (*diakoneō*) him, as Ignatius wanted to keep the *diakonos* Burrhus with him; Paul is "refreshed" by Philemon's love (Phlm 7; cf. 20); the love of the Ephesians refreshed

---

42. Wansink, *Chained in Christ*, 195; see Knox, *Philemon*, 53. The relevance of Knox's work to the present study will be discussed in chap. 5.

43. http://www.newadvent.org/fathers/0104.htm. Italics added.

Ignatius.[44] The name of the bishop (Onesimus of Ephesus) named at the head of the list of supporters in *Eph* 1.2 recalls the central figure in Paul's letter.[45] As Wansink observes: "Each prisoner responds to a church's having refreshed them. Each prisoner asks for the services of a 'slave'. Each prisoner sees the 'slave' as a representative of a particular church community."[46] The intertextual echoes underline the similarity between Onesimus and Burrhus as emissaries. If, as is at least possible, the bishop Onesimus of *Ephesians* were the same person as the Onesimus of Philemon, as church tradition holds, the "sent slave" (*servus emissarius*) hypothesis would be even stronger.

In chapter 2, I suggested that due to Paul's usage of the term *diakoneō* to describe Onesimus' "service" to him (Phlm 13), Onesimus could be counted as one of the few "deacons" named in the NT (with the due disclaimer that the term was not yet used to refer to an order of ministry): "a liaison officer in affairs of the gospel."[47] He is also, as T. Nicklas observes, an early instance of ancient Christian care for prisoners:

> Although it is doubtful that Onesimus was a runaway-slave (cf. Lampe 1985)—in such an instance, meeting Paul in prison would have simply been too dangerous—his concrete legal status is not completely clear. . . . The text indicates that Paul may have baptised Onesimus in prison (v. 10) and sent him back to his master Philemon (v. 12), even though Paul would have preferred to have Onesimus stay with him and serve him in prison. In other words, Philemon's διακονία is something Paul the prisoner could expect (v. 13; cf. also v. 20).[48]

---

44. Wansink, *Chained in Christ*, 196.

45. Wansink, *Chained in Christ*, 197. This Onesimus may or may not be the same person as the one named in Paul's letter; this is an issue that will be taken up in chapter 5.

46. Wansink, *Chained in Christ*, 197.

47. Collins, *Diakonia*, 222.

48. Nicklas, "Care for Prisoners," 56. Reference is to Peter Lampe, "Keine 'Sklavenflucht.'"

Niklas attributes the *diakonia* to Philemon, in the sense that the slave served as the slaveholder's proxy, but in real life, it was Onesimus who did the ministering in difficult and dangerous circumstances. In addition to the NT references to prison visitation mentioned above, Nicklas finds several pieces of early evidence of early Christian prison ministry, including the example from Ignatius cited above.[49] In addition to the example of Burrhus, Ignatius mentioned "a certain Philon, a Cilician deacon who assists Ignatius (*Phil.* 11:1; *Smyrn.* 10:1) and, along with a certain Theus/ Rheus Agathopus, clearly accompanies Ignatius from Antioch."[50] In the apocryphal Acts, which although not historical, reflect salient aspects of the social world in which they were written, Thecla is shown bribing a gatekeeper and a jailor so that she can meet Paul (*Paul and Thecla* 18).[51] Other women portrayed visiting Paul in the Acts are Artemilla and Ebula (*Acts of Paul* 7–8); the wife of the judge Ageates is portrayed as spending time with the imprisoned Andrew (*Acts of Andrew* 3–4; cf. *Passion of Andrew* 28–30).[52] A major piece of evidence is from the *Martyrdom of Perpetua and Felicity*, where two deacons intervene to improve the living conditions of imprisoned Christians:

> After a few days we are taken into the dungeon, and I was very much afraid, because I had never felt such darkness. O terrible day! O the fierce heat of the shock of the soldiery, because of the crowds! I was very unusually distressed by my anxiety for my infant. There were present there Tertius and Pomponius, the blessed deacons who ministered to us, and had arranged by means of a gratuity that we might be refreshed by being sent out for a few hours into a pleasanter part of the prison. (3.7)

More early evidence is cited by Canavan:

---

49. Nicklas, "Care for Prisoners," 58.
50. Nicklas, "Care for Prisoners," 58.
51. Nicklas, "Care for Prisoners," 59.
52. See Wansink, *Chained in Christ*, 81–82.

During the persecutions, special alms, at the instiga-
tion of the Bishops, were collected for those who were
sentenced to the quarries; and Pius I in A.D. 142 orders
the Bishop of Vienne to visit the prisons of the saints.
"If a Christian," say the Apostolic Constitutions [51], "is
condemned by the pagans to the amphitheatre or the
quarries for the name or the love of Jesus Christ, do
not abandon him to a disdainful forgetfulness. Take, as
the result of your labour and sweat, food and money to
soften the brutality of the warders, and to alleviate the
dreadful condition of your brother." . . . The law of Licin-
ius forbade these visits to the prisons; but still the Christians came, bringing their doles of food and money,
their happy and encouraging talk; striking from a man
like Lucian . . . a cry of genuine admiration that they
could be met so consistently at the prison gates when
they ran the risk of undergoing the cruelty of the mines
if they were apprehended in succouring those whom the
state had condemned.[53]

The impression that this kind of prison outreach was not unusual but regarded as a self-evident duty of the *ecclesia* is reinforced
by Lucian's *Death of Peregrinus* 12, mentioned earlier, that shows
Christians giving their imprisoned philosopher round-the-clock
care, including bribes from church officials.[54] Wansink agrees: "The
early Christians saw prison visitation as particularly important.
Tradition even has the admonition to visit the imprisoned back
as far as Jesus himself [Matt 25:36–44]."[55] The practice became so
entrenched that Cyprian (c. 250 CE) advised deacons and presby-
ters to instruct their parishioners to visit prisoners in small groups,
rather than in crowds, in order not to arouse suspicion among the
authorities (*Ep.* 4.2).[56] Tertullian went so far as to mock believers who provided "cookshops in the prisons" for "untrustworthy

53. Canavan, "Charity in the Early Church," 68.
54. Canavan, "Charity in the Early Church," 61.
55. Wansink, *Chained in Christ*, 81.
56. Wansink, *Chained in Christ*, 81.

martyrs" who should be fasting (*De ieiunio adversus Psychicos* 12).[57] Krause traced the institutionalization of the Christian practice of care for prisoners into late antiquity.[58]

A striking feature of early Christian accounts of care for prisoners is the repeated mention of deacons as key agents in visiting and providing resources for incarcerated believers. Two of the NT figures named as prison visitors—Tychicus (Col 4:7; 6:21) and Epaphras (Col 1:7)[59]—are identified as *diakonoi*; Epaphroditus is designated by the roughly synonymous term *leitourgon* (Phil 2:25) (BDAG 591–92). Likewise Burrhus (Ignatius, *Eph.* 2.1–12), Philon (*Phil.* 11:1; *Smyrn.* 10:1), Tertius and Pomponius (*Perpetua and Felicity* 3, 6, 10). A variety of first- and second-century texts confirm that one of the duties of deacons was prison ministry. According to the *Didaskalia*, deacons visited the sick, the needy, and confessors in prison; their efforts should include bribing guards to secure better treatment for prisoners (iv.7). Specific services for prisoners provided by deacons in early Christian materials similarly include: bringing gifts (Phil 4:18); relaying news (Col 4:7; Eph 6:21; Col 1:7; cf. *Perpetua and Felicity* 6); bearing letters (*Acts of Paul* 8; cf. Rom 16:1–2); accompanying those in custody on their way to prison (Ignatius; cf. *Perpetua and Felicity* 10, where the deacon Pomponius appears to Perpetua in a vision and accompanies her from the door of the prison to the arena); and, as in the *Didaskalia*, bribing guards (*Perpetua and Felicity* 13). If the "officials" mentioned by Lucian included deacons (*Peregrinus* 12), one of the favors gained through bribes was permission to spend the night with Christian prisoners. These disparate references give us a sense of the kinds of *diakonia* Onesimus may have offered the imprisoned Paul as he ferried amenities, messages, and

57. Wansink, *Chained in Christ*, 83.

58. Krause, *Gefängnisse im Römischen Reich*. Nicklas summarizes Krause's findings in "Care for Prisoners," 50.

59. Although Epaphras is a contraction of the name Epaphroditus, it is unlikely that the two names as they occur in the NT refer to the same person. Epaphras is named as Paul's fellow-prisoner in Phlm 23, so it's unlikely that he was the Epaphroditus who served as an emissary between Philippi and the apostle during his imprisonment in Ephesus (Phil 2:25; 4:18).

perhaps even bribes between the local *ecclesia* and the prisoner during his sojourn in Ephesus,[60] in addition to the emotional support offered by most prison visitors: "For a few days, then, we were comforted by the visits of our brethren. The consolation and the joy of the day removed all the agony we endured at night" (*Martyrdom of Saints Montanus and Lucius* 4.7).[61]

60. It is noteworthy that neither Philemon nor Philippians mentions Ephesus (or Rome for that matter), perhaps indicating that there was some strain between Paul and the local church. However, it makes much more sense to imagine that if Paul's language of birthing Onesimus referred to baptism (v. 10), the ritual took place in the local *ecclesia* rather than in prison. Further, it seems likely that Onesimus would have stayed with a member of the Ephesian church, rather than living in rented quarters.

61. Quoted by Wansink, *Chained in Christ*, 83.

# 5

# The Faithful and Beloved Brother

DESPITE BEING THE ADDRESSEE of Paul's only authentic personal letter, Philemon is not mentioned elsewhere in his correspondence, or anywhere else in the New Testament. Somewhat surprisingly, Onesimus is. The final greeting in Col 4:7–9 mentions that Onesimus ("the faithful and beloved brother, who is one of you," v. 9) will return to Colossae with a missionary named Tychicus: "they will tell you about everything here." Note the use of the plural—"*they* will tell you everything." The scenario is that Onesimus, still enslaved, is travelling back to Colossae with Tychicus for his uneasy reunion with Philemon. Nonetheless, the writer assumes that *both* Tychicus (presumably free) and Onesimus (still enslaved) will inform the *ecclesia* concerning Paul's wishes. Like Philemon, Colossians is a prison letter (4:3, 10, 18), but unlike Philemon, it is regarded by many scholars as Deutero-Pauline: written by a follower of Paul after the apostle's death. Whoever wrote the letter regarded Onesimus (along with other figures mentioned in Phlm 23: Epaphras [1:7], Archippus [4:17]; Aristarchus and Mark [4:10], Luke and Demas [4:14]) as important enough to remember as Paul's trusted emissary.

John Knox has been mentioned in previous chapters as one of the first critical scholars to challenge the traditional narrative of Onesimus as a runaway slave. Knox argued that it was much more likely that Onesimus was sent by his master Archippus (not Philemon) to assist Paul in prison; Paul addressed Philemon first because as a church leader in Laodicea (not Colossae), he would have had some authority to persuade Archippus to release Onesimus for Paul's service.[1] Building on the work of E. J. Goodspeed,[2] Knox posited that Colossians, which he accepted as authentic, was written as a companion-letter to Philemon, which is the "letter from Laodicea" mentioned in Colossians (Col 4:16; cf. 4:13, 15), presumably brought by Tychicus and Onesimus for circulation among the churches in the Lycus valley at Colossae, Laodicea, and Hierapolis (Col 4:13).[3] After Paul's death, Ephesians, an expansion of Colossians, was written as a cover-letter for a collection of Paul's letters,[4] which included Philemon as an appendix to Colossians. This accounts for the inclusion of Philemon, a brief and ostensibly insignificant letter,[5] in the Pauline corpus, and, ultimately, in the NT canon.

As mentioned in chapter 4, Knox takes Goodspeed's reconstruction further by positing that the Onesimus, bishop of Ephesus, mentioned in Ignatius' *Letter to the Ephesians* (1, 2, 6) was the Onesimus of Philemon. Many contemporary scholars doubt this identification—Onesimus was a common name in antiquity, and Paul's Onesimus would have been very old by the time Ignatius wrote *Ephesians* (c. 110).[6] However, it's not impossible; if, as suggested earlier, Onesimus was a young man when he met Paul (c. 55 CE), he might have been in his early seventies by Ignatius' time. A more serious objection to Knox's (and Goodspeed's) reconstruction is that Colossians is now widely regarded as inauthentic, although this could be accounted for by supposing that Colossians was written by a Pauline disciple (among other things) to recognize the discipleship of Onesimus, while at the same time ensuring that other believing slaves would not expect to be accorded the same

---

1. Knox, *Philemon*, 29–34.

2. Goodspeed, *New Solutions of New Testament Problems*, 52–58.

3. Knox, *Philemon*, 13–24.

4. Knox, *Philemon*, 35–45.

5. Knox, *Philemon*, 46.

6. Holmes, *Apostolic Fathers*, 90.

special treatment as Paul's protégé.[7] Ironically, the teaching that slaves should obey their masters "according to the flesh" (Col 3:22; Eph 6:5) has been used by generations of Christian slaveholders to justify the institution of slavery.[8]

Whether or not the Onesimus who attended Paul in prison and the bishop of Ephesus were the same person, Wansink's observations about the intertextual echoes between Philemon and *Ephesians* hold: "Ignatius exploits the fact that an important reader of his epistle would have been the community's bishop, a man by the name of Onesimus. Regardless whether this was the same man who was with Paul in prison, Ignatius shapes his letter as if this community, or this bishop, would have been familiar with echoes of Paul's letter to Philemon."[9] In Knox's historicizing interpretation, it was Onesimus of Ephesus who oversaw the writing of Ephesians and the collection of the Pauline letters. Although (like many scholars), he does not accept Knox's reconstruction, Robert Seesengood admits that his reading is workable: "It accounts for much of the data and produces a reasonable and plausible historical reconstruction that also resonates with some of the received Christian traditions."[10] Thus, in a Onesimus-centered approach like this one, it would be remiss not to mention it. At the very least, it suggests that the early *ecclesia* remembered Onesimus as a faithful and trustworthy disciple who carried on his *diakonia* for decades after Paul's death. Whether or not Onesimus the bishop and Paul's disciple were the same person, it is plausible from his name that Onesimus of Ephesus was a freedman as opposed to freeborn. Significantly, Ignatius, who advocated a strongly hierarchical church polity,[11] had no compunction about aligning the bishop and the slave.[12]

7. Knox, *Philemon*, 17.

8. See Beavis, "Slaves Obey Your Masters"; Wedow, "Servants Obey Your Masters".

9. Wansink, "Chained in Christ," 195.

10. Seesengood, *Philemon*, 63.

11. Homes, *Apostolic Fathers*, 88–89.

12. An instance of a bishop—in fact, a pope—with a servile background is

Historical questions aside, church tradition has consistently identified the bishop of Ephesus (also known as Onesimus of Byzantium) with the Onesimus of Philemon (see Figure 3). Hanson reports that "St. Onesimus, as a celebrated New Testament figure and patron of servants and slaves, was venerated in many areas Europe and the Near East. Such veneration was especially strong in Byzantium. Constantinople itself possessed two churches dedicated to the Saint, as well a most cherished relic: the hand of Onesimus."[13] The fourth-century *Apostolic Canons* (82) cites Onesimus as a precedent for the ordination of the enslaved, affirming that Philemon both forgave and manumitted Onesimus: "We do not permit servants to be ordained into the clergy without their masters' consent; for this would grieve those that owned them. For such a practice would occasion the subversion of families. But if at any time a servant appears worthy to be ordained into an high office, such as our Onesimus appeared to be, and if his master allows of it, and gives him his freedom, and dismisses him from his house, let him be ordained."[14] As Hanson observes, "Onesimus did figure prominently in the ecclesiastical and hagiographical traditions of early Christianity, while his cultus seems to have enjoyed some prominence during the Middle Ages."[15] Hanson cites a varied hagiographical tradition in which Onesimus variously served as bishop of the Macedonian city of Beroea, worked as an itinerant preacher in Spain, and, depending on the source, was martyred in Colossae under Nero, at Rome under Trajan, or in Puteoli under Domitian.[16] Like other ha-

---

Callixtus I (r. 218–22), although the account of his scandalous career in Hippolytus' *Refutation of All Heresies* 9 was likely intended to smear the reputation of a bishop the author regarded as a heretic (Flexsenhar, *Christians in Caesar's Household*, 61–70). Interestingly, Hippolytus' stereotypical portrayal of Callixtus as a thief and a runaway resembles the "runaway slave" hypothesis initiated by Chrysostom. For a less skeptical appraisal of Callixtus, see Bradley, *Slavery and Society*, 146–47.

13. Hanson, "Passion of Onesimus," 350 n. 5. His feast day in the Orthodox church is February 16; February 15 in the Roman calendar.

14. https://www.ccel.org/ccel/schaff/anf07.ix.ix.vi.html, April 24, 2020.

15. Hanson, "Passion of Onesimus," 135.

16. Hanson, "Passion of Onesimus," 351–52. For references, see his notes

giographies, the Onesimus traditions were "principally concerned with transmitting the 'higher' truth of the Christian God to [their] audience, . . . [and] understandably utilized the transient 'historical' events of the material world as convenient backdrops for the larger drama of Good vs. Evil."[17]

Figure 3: Icon of Onesimus

19–24.

17. Hanson, "Greek Martyrdom Account," 323.

The earliest extant account of Onesimus' martyrdom is in a preface to the letters of Paul written by the deacon Euthalius (c. 400), which states that after many labors, Onesimus was martyred in Rome under the prefect Tertullus; his legs were broken in the process, a motif that endures in his iconography (see Figure 4).[18] The Puteoli tradition, elaborated in the *Struggle of the Holy Apostle Onesimus, Disciple of the Holy Head Apostle Paul* (750–800), conflates the biblical Onesimus with another martyr by that name (Onesimus Leontinis), who was martyred, along with three brothers he had instructed in the faith, during the Valerian persecution (258–60).[19] Here, Onesimus is arrested and tried for evangelizing the wife of the prefect Tertullus. He is described as: "the one who brought over the theology and true word of Paul to make known his [Paul's] advocacy on behalf of him in a letter, the one to Philemon, his master."[20] Hanson summarizes its content:

> [T]he outstanding feature of the martyrdom account is the discourse and exhortation by Onesimus during his initial interrogation in Rome. After confessing his Christian faith before Tertullus, Onesimus launches into an impressive and lengthy denunciation of the lurking evils of his contemporary world. The use made of simile, metaphor and personification in this section is particularly striking. Onesimus devotes a great part of his discourse to a condemnation of Roman paganism and makes a number of allusions to various Roman cults and cult practices. No doubt, the author drew much his material for this "idolatry" section from the apologetic writings of the Greek Fathers, especially Athanasius and Clement. Onesimus concludes his eloquent defense by calling Tertullus to abandon his idols and sinful ways, and to follow the precepts of the Christian God.[21]

18. Hanson, "Passion of Onesimus," 352.

19. Hanson, "Passion of Onesimus," 353.

20. Hanson, "Greek Martyrdom Account," 327.

21. Hanson, "Passion of Onesimus," 357. The Greek text of the *Passion* is included on pp. 368–74 of Hanson's article. For English translation, see Hanson, "Greek Martyrdom Account," 325–39.

Hanson cautions that despite these vivid martyrdom tales, only one early source (Euthalius, cited above) reports that Onesimus was martyred.[22]

Elizabeth Castelli has argued that the figure of the martyr has become overly aligned with the semantic field of suffering and self-sacrifice, and calls for a focus on the dimension of martyrdom that privileges "witnessing, truth-telling, testimony."[23] In Onesimus' passion narrative, which admittedly dwells on the torments suffered by him and his fellow believers,[24] more space is devoted to an account of his testimony to the eparch Tertullus.[25] Although the testimony was composed centuries after the death of Onesimus, slave or bishop, theologically, it coheres well with the authentic teachings of a fifth-century bishop with enslavement in his biography, Patrick of Ireland: a strong sense of the sinfulness of the world (*Conf.* 1); condemnation of idolatry (*Conf.* 38, 41); the conviction that the Christian God is the sole source of salvation (*Conf.* 1, 2). For the purposes of this study, it is worth noting that Onesimus is remembered in the most elaborated account of his significance as one who "lightened his [Paul's] chains by his arrival, cheered the dejected by his presence, and lessened the pains by his physical ministries [*sōmatikais diakoniais*] to the apostolic body"[26]—as disciple, deacon, apostle, bishop, witness, and saint.

---

22. Hanson, "Passion of Onesimus," 352.

23. Castelli, *Martyrdom and Memory*, 203.

24. Hanson, "Greek Martyrdom Account," 335–39. *Struggle* II.100–208.

25. Hanson, "Greek Martyrdom Account," 329–35. *Struggle* II.218–275.

26. Hanson, "Greek Martyrdom Account," 328, 329. *Struggle* I.80.

Figure 4: Saint Onesimus the Apostle

# A Man of Inexpressible Love

> I received, therefore, your whole multitude in the name
> of God, through Onesimus, a man of inexpressible love,
> and your bishop in the flesh, whom I pray you by Jesus
> Christ to love, and that you would all seek to be like him.
> And blessed be He who has granted unto you, being wor-
> thy, to obtain such an excellent bishop.[1]

BIBLICAL SCHOLARS HAVE LONG neglected the figure of Onesimus,
but creative writers have shown some fascination with his story.[2]
This afterword does not set out to provide a fictionalized biography of Onesimus, but to imagine his perspective on the letter Paul
wrote on his behalf, informed by the biographical discourses of the
formerly enslaved (italicized),[3] both ancient (Patrick, Epictetus,
Aesop, Hermas) and modern (Lorenzo Ivy, Frederick Douglass,
Venture Smith, Louis Hughes, Moses Roper, Vilet Lester, Mary
Prince, Harriet Jacobs, Sojourner Truth).

---

1. Ignatius, *Eph.* 1. Roberts and Donaldson, trans., *Ante-Nicene Fathers* 1,
https://www.newadvent.org/fathers/0104.htm, accessed April 28, 2020.

2. E.g., Abbot, *Onesimus—Memoirs of a Disciple of St. Paul*; McDowell, *Onesimus: A Novel*; Potter, *Onesimus: The Prince and the Slave*; Jones, *Onesimus,
the Run-Away Slave*.

3. And a few related texts.

## A Memoir of Onesimus

When it comes to the retelling of my story, *The half has never been told.*[4] *Although I am imperfect in many ways, I want my brothers and relations to know what I'm really like, so that they can see what it is that inspires my life.*[5] I was born in the household of Philemon. My mother's name was Rhoda. She was sold while I was still very young. I'm not sure of my exact age; I think I was less than twenty when Paul wrote his letter about me. *By far the larger part of the slaves know as little of their ages as horses know of theirs, and it is the wish of most masters within my knowledge to keep their slaves thus ignorant. I do not remember to have ever met a slave who could tell of his birthday. They seldom come nearer to it than planting-time, harvest-time, cherry-time, spring-time, or fall-time. A want of information concerning my own was a source of unhappiness to me, even during childhood.*[6]

Because I was young and quite strong, I was chosen to travel to Ephesus in the company of my master's friend Tychicus to bring food, clothing, and money to a teacher named Paul, who had visited his house a few times. I was a hard worker. *I was pretty much employed in the house at carding wool and other household business. In this situation I continued for some years, after which my master put me to work out of doors. After many proofs of my faithfulness and honesty, my master began to put great confidence in me. My behavior to him had as yet been submissive and obedient. I then began to have hard tasks imposed on me. Some of these were to pound four bushels of ears of corn every night in a barrel for the poultry, or be rigorously punished. At other seasons of the year I had to card wool*[7] *until a very late hour. These tasks I had to perform when I was about nine years old.*[8] The family business was the textile trade,[9]

4. Lorenzo Ivy.

5. Patrick, *Confessio* 6. Trans. O'Loughlin, *Patrick.*

6. Frederick Douglass, *Narrative of the Life of Frederick Douglass*, 1.

7 This refers to the preparation of wool fiber for spinning.

8. Venture Smith, *Life and Adventures of Venture*, 15.

9. Cadwallader, "Onesimus," 598.

so my master was quite well off. I was taught to read and write so that I could help with inventory and accounts, another reason why master chose me to go to Paul. I took some pride in being chosen to do an errand in another city, even though waiting on a political prisoner was dangerous—too dangerous for master himself to risk. They say that slaves have no honor, but I felt that I had some when I was ordered to go to all the way to Ephesus to help Paul—a free man, but, as a prisoner, less free that I was, at the time. *Few privileges were esteemed higher, by the slaves of the out-farms, than that of being selected to do errands. . . . It was associated in their minds with greatness. . . . They regarded it as evidence of great confidence reposed in them by their overseers; and it was on this account, as well as a constant desire to be out of the field from under the driver's lash, that they esteemed it a high privilege, one worth careful living for. He was called the smartest and most trusty fellow, who had this honor conferred upon him the most frequently.*[10]

A few years before, master had stopped worshipping at the household *lararium* and started hosting thanksgiving meals with the family and some of his friends and neighbors in honor of a god called Kyrios Christos. Some of us slaves helped serve the meals and cleaned up afterwards. If we were lucky, we got to eat some of the leftovers. Master made everyone in the household go through a water ritual, but it didn't make much difference to us slaves. *His slaves thinking him a very bad sample of what a professing Christian ought to be, would not join the connection he belonged to, thinking they must be a very bad set of people.*[11] Some of their preaching was directed to us. *You out to heared that preachin'. Obey your massa and missy, don't steal chickens and eggs and meat, but nary a word 'bout havin' a soul to slave. . . . Church was what they called it, but all that preacher talked about was for us slaves to obey our masters and not to lie and steal. Nothing about Jesus was ever said. How could anybody be converted on dat kind of preachin'?*[12] Some of us took it to heart—it's what we'd heard all our lives, so didn't really

10. Douglass, *Narrative of the Life of Frederick Douglass*, 12–13.

11. Roper, *Adventures and Escape of Moses Roper*, 30.

12. Elkins, *Slavery Remembered*, 114.

question that God was a master who wanted us to be obedient slaves—but others saw through it. *Yet she now sees very clearly the false position they were all in, both masters and slaves; and she looks back, with utter astonishment, at the absurdity of the claims so arrogantly set up by the masters, over beings designed by God to be as free as kings; and at the perfect stupidity of the slave, in admitting for one moment the validity of these claims.*[13]

There is a rumor going around that I was a runaway, and even that I was a thief. Typical—that's the way the freeborn always talk about slaves. They never understand that *the condition of a slave confuses all principles of morality, and, in fact, renders the practice of them impossible.*[14] Sure, sometimes slaves take things their masters can easily do without to fill our bellies or make our lives more comfortable—goodness knows, we've earned it. I can't say that I never thought of running away—most of us have. But I was afraid to, and I didn't want to leave my partner Arethusa and her baby. *Aren't you ashamed to be more cowardly and ignoble than a runaway slave? How do they, when they run off, leave their masters? In what estates or slaves do they put their confidence? Don't they steal just a little bit to last them for the first few days, and then afterwards drift along over land or sea, contriving one scheme after another to keep themselves fed?*[15] I heard a story from Aesop, who was once a slave himself, that makes the point that even if you run away, you might end up even worse off, working in the mines on a treadmill. *When, after a long time, a man caught sight of his runaway slave and pursued him, the slave fled into a mill for refuge; whereupon the master said, "Where would I rather have found you than here?"*[16] I know some of these old stories are made up to keep us from getting ideas, but there's some truth to them. Like this one: *A slave running away from a master of cruel disposition met Aesop, to whom he was known as a neighbor. "What are you excited about?" asked Aesop.*

13. Sojourner Truth and Olive Gilbert, *Narrative of Sojourner Truth*, 34–35.

14. Jacobs, *Incidents in the Life of a Slave Girl*, 85.

15. Epictetus, *Discourses* 3.26. (Oldfather trans.).

16. Perry, trans., *Babrius and Phaedrus*, 510. The anthologist Phaedrus was a freedman.

*"I will tell you frankly, father—and you deserve to be called by that name—since my complaint can be safely entrusted to your keeping. I get a surplus of blows and a shortage of rations. Every now and then I am sent out to my master's farm without any provisions for the journey. Whenever he dines at home I stand by in attendance all night long; if he is invited out I lie in the street until daybreak. I have earned my liberty, but I am still a slave though gray-headed. If I were aware of any fault on my own part, I should bear this with patience. I have never yet had my belly full, and besides that I have the bad luck to suffer tyranny exercised by a cruel master. For these reasons, and others which it would be too long to recount, I have decided to go away wherever my feet shall take me." "Now then, listen," said Aesop, "these are the hardships that you suffer, according to your account, when you have done no wrong; what if you commit an offence? What do you think you will suffer then?" By such advice the man was de-*terred from running away.*[17] But I don't agree that a freed slave is worse off than one still in slavery, as some philosophers I've heard of say. *A slave wishes to be immediately set free. Think you it is because he is desirous to pay his fee [of manumission] to the officer? No, but because he fancies that, for want of acquiring his freedom, he has hitherto lived under restraint and unprosperously. "If I am once set free," he says, "it is all prosperity; I care for no one; I can speak to all as being their equal and on a level with them. I go where I will, I come when and how I will." He is at last made free, and presently having nowhere to eat he seeks whom he may flatter, with whom he may sup. He then either submits to the basest and most infamous degradation, and if he can obtain admission to some great man's table, falls into a slavery much worse than the former; or perhaps, if the ignorant fellow should grow rich, he doats upon some girl, laments, and is unhappy, and wishes for slavery again. "For what harm did it do me? Another clothed me, another shod me, another fed me, another took care of me when I was sick. It was but in a few things, by way of return, I used to serve him. But now, miserable wretch! what do I suffer, in being a slave to many, instead of one!"*[18] I wanted to

17. Perry, trans., *Babrius and Phaedrus*, 401.

18. Epictetus, *Discourses* 4.1.35–37. http://www.perseus.tufts.edu/hopper/

be legally manumitted someday. I though maybe if I worked hard and saved up some money, I could buy myself out first, and later Arethusa and the baby. *At the close of that year I was sold . . . and had to be separated from my wife and one daughter, who was about one month old. [My new owner] resided at Stonington-point. To this place I brought with me from my late master's, two johannes, three old Spanish dollars, and two thousand of coppers, besides five pounds of my wife's money. This money I got by cleaning gentlemen's shoes and drawing boots, by catching musk-rats and minks, raising potatoes and carrots, &c. and by fishing in the night, and at odd spells. . . . I asked my master one time if he would consent to have me purchase my freedom. He replied that he would. I was then very happy, knowing that I was at that time able to pay part of the purchase money, by means of the money which I some time since buried. . . . [B]eing in my forty-fourth year, I purchased my wife Meg, and thereby prevented having another child to buy, as she was then pregnant. I gave forty pounds for her.*[19] Most of us slaves hope to be manumitted someday, but for most of us, it never happens.

I felt sorry for Paul when I first met him; he was so hungry and thin and dirty. He pretended not to be scared, but I know he was. I could sympathize; sometimes master punished us by confining us in a dark pit until he felt like letting us out again and it seemed like forever, but we knew that we'd likely be let out before too long. Paul didn't know what was ahead of him. He appreciated the food, water, and clean clothes I was able to bring him. *I was confined here in a dungeon underground, the grating of which looked to the door of the gaoler's house. His wife had a great antipathy to me. . . . My grandmother used to come to me nearly every day, and bring me something to eat, besides the regular gaol allowance, by which my sufferings were somewhat decreased.*[20] Since it was what I was sent to do, I spent as much time as I could with Paul, or just waiting outside with other visitors. The Ephesians didn't visit him much, as they were afraid of being arrested themselves,

text?doc=Perseus%3Atext%3A1999.01.0237%3Atext%3Ddisc%3Abook%3D4.

19. Smith, *Life of Venture*, 18, 22, 27.

20. Roper, *Life and Adventures of Moses Roper*, 21.

but they sent messages and supplies with me, and Paul gave me messages to take back to them. They even gave me money to bribe the soldier he was chained to, to let me spend extra time with him. I certainly lived up to my name!

Paul told me some of the stories of his people, who were once slaves in Egypt. They even had a law that a runaway slave should be sheltered, not sent back to his master. *I was told afterwards, that some of those men who took me were professing Christians, but, to me, they did not seem to live up to what they professed; they did not seem, by their practice, at least, to recognize that God as their God, who hath said, "thou shalt not deliver unto his master, the servant which is escaped from his master unto thee, he shall dwell with thee, even among you, in that place which he shall choose, in one of thy gates, where it liketh him best; thou shalt not oppress him."—Deut. xxiii:15, 16.*[21] When I wasn't with him, a member of the *ecclesia* in the city kept me in the slave quarters in his house.

Paul has a saying that it doesn't matter whether you're a man or a woman, Jew or Greek, slave or free—it's all the same for the brothers and sisters. I really like that, although the believers don't always live up to it. Because I'd gone through the water ritual at Philemon's house, the Ephesians let me share in their early-morning worship. Sometimes they'd even wait on the slaves as a symbol of our unity. *In heaven's kingdom the free will serve the slaves and the attendants of the bridal chamber will serve the wedding guests.*[22] After the meal, though, we went back into our old roles, and got the usual slave rations. *He fed the children [baked] bread [and meat]. He fed the slaves [oil and] grain. [He fed] the cattle barley, chaff, and fodder.*[23]

I helped Paul write his letter to Philemon. Paul had only met my master a few times; I knew him all too well. Household slaves like me have to pay attention to master and mistress's every whim, or we get in trouble. *I got along for the first two weeks very nicely.*

21. Roper, *Life and Adventures of Moses Roper*, 21.

22. *Gos. Phil.* 72; Marvin Meyer translation, http://gnosis.org/naghamm/GPhilip-Meyer.html, accessed April 27, 2020.

23. *Gos. Phil.* 81.

*I gave them satisfaction, as I thought; they, that is my master and his wife, appeared pleased. I concluded I was all right and was going to have a nice time at my new home. At this time there was not the dread of a daily whipping and the loss of one meal a day. It was not long before I was to learn that storms followed calms, and war came after peace. . . . My heart sank within me. What good was it for me to try to please? She would find fault anyway. Her usual morning greeting was: "Well, Lou, have you dusted the parlors?" "Oh, yes," I would answer. "Have the flowers been arranged?" "Yes, all is in readiness," I would say. Once I had stoned the steps as usual, but the madam grew angry as soon as she saw them. I had labored hard, and thought she would be pleased. The result, however, was very far from that. She took me out, stripped me of my shirt and began thrashing me, saying I was spoiled. I was no longer a child, but old enough to be treated differently. I began to cry, for it seemed to me my heart would break. But, after the first burst of tears, the feeling came over me that I was a man, and it was an outrage to treat me so—to keep me under the lash day after day.*[24] I knew that the letter was about me, so it was important to me that it be written in just the right way. In fact, although Paul dictated the letter, I was the one who actually wrote it down until he ended it in his own hand, so that my master wouldn't think I'd forged it. Philemon has a strong sense of honor and pride in being the head of a household, running a successful business, and being well off enough to host an ecclesia in his house. I told Paul it would be a good idea to compliment him on his faithfulness and love for God and the brothers and sisters, and for his partnership in faith with Paul. *I hav long bin wishing to imbrace this presant and pleasant opertunity of unfolding my Seans and fealings Since I was constrained to leav my Long Loved home and friends which I cannot never gave my Self the Least promis of returning to.*[25] Asking him outright would be a mistake—Paul could drop some strong hints, but Master would have to make the decision. *The Epistle of Paul to Philemon is the most pregnant of compositions. Never was so much meaning compressed*

---

24. Hughes, *Thirty Years a Slave*, 73–74.
25. Vilet Lester, Letter, August 29, 1857.

*into so few words. And then, how weighty the topics. How much
of doctrine is there in those few verses; how much of history. And
the doctrine and the history are so presented, that while you cannot
deny the history, you are encouraged to receive the doctrine. The
letter is a series of implications;—implied facts, implied principles,
implied duties, implied changes and triumphs, set forth in all the
unconscious simplicity of a private and confidential communication, so as to conciliate attention and win belief. I hold this short
Epistle to be of itself an antidote to scepticism and a confutation of
slavery.*[26] After all, the whole idea was to ask him to devote me to
Paul's service full-time, not just as a loan, but as a gift. I've heard
that serving two masters can be a lot worse than just one. *Some
time after I had another difficulty and oppression which was greater
than any I had ever experienced since I came into this country. This
was to serve two masters.*[27] I was a bit offended when Paul called
me "useless"—he'd heard master call me that when he was angry
at me, although I was nothing of the kind. If I was so useless, why
was Philemon so anxious for Paul to send me back? (Of course,
he blamed me for the delay, but Paul just didn't want to part with
me.) Why would Paul profit by Philemon's gifting me to him? But
if it helped make up Philemon's mind to grant his request, I could
take it (I'd taken a lot worse!). Paul hoped to be released soon and
wanted me to travel with him if master agreed to send me back. I
hoped so too, but who knew? God, I guess. Anyway, Paul needed
me more that Philemon did, and he was very grateful for everything I did for him—even just for my company.

As I said before, Paul's teaching about the good news made
more sense to me than anything I'd heard in Colossae, and he ex-
plained the reason why I'd gone through that *baptizmos* in Philemon's house—it was a kind of rebirth into a new life. Because he's
the one who brought me to faith, Paul calls me his child who was
born in chains, like the babes whose poor mothers give birth to
them in prison. I don't think it occurred to him at the time that as
a slave, I had been born in bondage. *I was born at Brackish-Pond,*

26. Beard, *Life of Toussaint L'Ouverture*, 42–43.
27. Smith, *Life of Venture Smith*, 15. Cf. Matt 6:24.

*in Bermuda, on a farm belonging to Mr. Charles Myners. My mother was a household slave; and my father, whose name was Prince, was a sawyer belonging to Mr. Trimmingham, a ship-builder at Crow-Lane. When I was an infant, old Mr. Myners died, and there was a division of the slaves and other property among the family.*[28] But since I barely knew my mother, and have no idea who my father was, it means a lot to me that someone like Paul would see me as his child. I'd heard that it's possible for a master to adopt a slave as his own son if he doesn't have an heir. *A certain man had a field and many slaves, and he planted a certain part of the field with a vineyard, and selecting a faithful and beloved and much valued slave, he called him to him, and said, "Take this vineyard which I have planted, and stake it until I come, and do nothing else to the vineyard; and attend to this order of mine, and you shall receive your freedom from me." And the master of the slave departed to a foreign country. And when he was gone, the slave took and staked the vineyard; and when he had finished the staking of the vines, he saw that the vineyard was full of weeds. He then reflected, saying, "I have kept this order of my master: I will dig up the rest of this vineyard, and it will be more beautiful when dug up; and being free of weeds, it will yield more fruit, not being choked by them." He took, therefore, and dug up the vineyard, and rooted out all the weeds that were in it. And that vineyard became very beautiful and fruitful, having no weeds to choke it. And after a certain time the master of the slave and of the field returned, and entered into the vineyard. And seeing that the vines were suitably supported on stakes, and the ground, moreover, dug up, and all the weeds rooted out, and the vines fruitful, he was greatly pleased with the work of his slave. And calling his beloved son who was his heir, and his friends who were his councillors, he told them what orders he had given his slave, and what he had found performed. And they rejoiced along with the slave at the testimony which his master bore to him. And he said to them, "I promised this slave freedom if he obeyed the command which I gave him; and he has kept my command, and done besides a good work to the vineyard, and has pleased me exceedingly. In*

28. Prince, *History of Mary Prince*, 1.

*return, therefore, for the work which he has done, I wish to make*
*him co-heir with my son, because, having good thoughts, he did*
*not neglect them, but carried them out." With this resolution of the*
*master his son and friends were well pleased, viz., that the slave*
*should be co-heir with the son.*[29] Paul never did legally adopt me
like the slave in that story, but after Philemon agreed to give me
to him as an offering to the mission, the apostle did give me my
freedom not just as a reward for my good service, but to show that
slave and free really are all one in Kyrios Christos.

Figure 5: Onesimus returns to Philemon with Paul's letter in his hands.

29. Hermas, *Similitudes* 5.2. http://www.earlychristianwritings.com/text/
shepherd.html, accessed April 28, 2020.

# Bibliography

Abbot, Edwin. *Onesimus—Memoirs of a Disciple of St. Paul*. Boston: Roberts Brothers, 1882.

Amerasingh, C. W. "The Part of the Slave in Terence's Drama." *Greece & Rome* 19.56 (1950) 62–72.

Artz-Grabner, Peter. *Philemon*. Papyrologishe Kommentar zum Neuen Testament Band 1. Göttingen: Vandenhoeck & Ruprecht, 2003.

Aymer, Margaret. "Outrageous, Audacious, Courageous, Wilful: Reading the Enslaved Girl of Acts 12." In *Womanist Interpretations of the Bible: Expanding the Discourse*, edited by Gay L. Byron and Vanessa Lovelace, 265–90. Atlanta: Society of Biblical Literature, 2016.

Barclay, John M. G. "Paul, Philemon and the Dilemma of Christian Slave-Ownership." *New Testament Studies* 37 (1991) 161–86.

Barnes, Albert. *An Inquiry into the Scriptural Views of Slavery*. Philadelphia: Perkins and Purvis, 1846.

Barth, Markus, and Helmut Blanke. *The Letter to Philemon: A New Translation with Notes and Commentary*. Grand Rapids: Eerdmans, 2000.

Batten, Alicia. "Philemon." In *Philippians, Colossians, Philemon*, by Elsa Tamez, Cynthia Briggs Kittredge, Claire Miller Colombo, and Alicia J. Batten, 201–64. Wisdom Commentaries. Collegeville, MN: Liturgical, 2017.

Beard, John Relly. *The Life of Toussaint L'Ouverture, The Negro Patriot of Hayti: Comprising an Account of the Struggle for Liberty in the Island and a Sketch of Its History to the Present Period*. London: Ingram, Cooke, and Co., 1853.

Beavis, Mary Ann "The Parable of the Slave, Son, and Vineyard: An Early Christian Freedman's Narrative (Hermas *Similitudes* 5.2–11)." *Catholic Biblical Quarterly* 80 (2018) 655–69.

———. "The Parable of the Talents (Matthew 25:14–30); Imagining a Slave's Perspective." *Journal of Gospels and Acts Research* 2 (2018) 7–21.

———. "Six Years a Slave: The *Confessio* of St. Patrick as Slave Narrative." *Irish Theological Quarterly* 85.4 (2020) 1–13.

————. "Slaves Obey Your Masters according to the Flesh (Col 3:22a; Eph 6:5a) in Servile Perspective." *Listening: Journal of Communication Ethics, Religion, and Culture,* forthcoming.

Benjamin, Walter. "Theses on the Philosophy of History." In *Illuminations,* translated by Harry Zohn, edited by Hannah Arendt, 253–63. New York: Schocken, 2011.

Berry, Daina Ramey. *The Price for Their Pound of Flesh: The Value of the Enslaved, from Womb to Grave, in the Building of a Nation.* Boston: Beacon, 2017.

Bieberstein, Sabine. "Disrupting the Normal Reality of Slavery: A Feminist Reading of the Letter to Philemon." *Journal for the Study of the New Testament* 79 (2000) 105–16.

Blassingame, John W. *The Slave Community: Plantation Life in the Antebellum South.* 1972. Reprint, New York: Oxford University Press, 1979.

————, ed. *Slave Testimony: Two Centuries of Letters, Speeches, Interviews, and Autobiographies.* Baton Rouge, LA: Louisiana State University Press, 1977.

Bodel, John. "Death and Social Death in Ancient Rome." In *On Human Bondage: After Slavery and Social Death,* edited by John Bodel and Walter Scheidel, 81–108. New York: Wiley, 2017.

Bömer, Franz. *Untersuchungen über die Religion der Sklaven in Griechenland und Rom.* 4 vols. Wiesbaden: Steiner, 1957, 1960, 1962, 1963.

Bradley, Keith. "The Bitter Chain of Slavery: Reflections on Slavery in Ancient Rome." http://nrs.harvard.edu/urn-3:hlnc.essay:BradleyK.The_Bitter_Chain_of_Slavery.2005.

————. "Engaging with Slavery." *Biblical Interpretation* 21 (2013) 533–46.

————. "Resisting Slavery at Rome." In *The Cambridge World History of Slavery: Volume 1: The Ancient Mediterranean World,* edited by Keith Bradley and Paul Cartledge, 362–84. Cambridge: Cambridge University Press, 2011.

————. "Roman Slavery and Roman Law." *Historical Reflections* 15.3 (1998) 477–95.

————. "Roman Slavery: Retrospect and Prospect." *Canadian Journal of History/Annales canadiennes d'histoire* 43 (2008) 478–500.

————. *Slaves and Masters in the Roman Empire: A Study of Social Control.* Oxford: Oxford University Press, 1984.

————. *Slavery and Society at Rome.* Key Themes in Ancient History. Cambridge: Cambridge University Press, 1994.

Briggs, Sheila. "The Labor of Freedpersons Is Never Free." Society of Biblical Literature Annual Meeting, San Diego, CA, November 23, 2019.

Brogdon, Lewis. *A Companion to Philemon.* Eugene, OR: Cascade, 2018.

Brown, Vincent. "Social Death and Political Life in the Study of Slavery." *American Historical Review* 114.5 (2009) 1231–49.

Cadwallader, Alan J. "Onesimus and the Social and Geographical World of Philemon." In *Lexham Geographic Commentary on Acts through Revelation,* edited by Barry J. Beitzel, 590–604. Bellingham, WA: Lexham, 2019.

Callahan, Allen Dwight. *Embassy of Onesimus: The Letter of Paul to Philemon.* The New Testament in Context. Valley Forge, PA: Trinity, 1997.

Canavan, Joseph E. "Charity in the Early Church." *Irish Quarterly Review* 12.45 (1923) 61–77.

Carrington, Philip. *The Early Christian Church.* Vol. 1. Cambridge: Cambridge University Press, 1957.

Cassidy, Richard J. *Paul in Chains: Roman Imprisonment and the Letter of St. Paul.* New York: Crossroad, 2001.

Castelli, Elizabeth. *Martyrdom and Memory: Early Christian Culture Making.* New York: Columbia University Press, 2007.

Charles, Ronald. *The Silencing of Slaves in Early Jewish and Christian Texts.* Routledge Studies in the Early Christian World. London: Routledge, 2020.

Collins, John N. *Diakonia: Re-Interpreting the Ancient Sources.* New York: Oxford University Press, 1990.

Dal Lago, Enrico, and Constantina Katsari. "The Study of Ancient and Modern Slave Systems: Setting an Agenda for Comparison." In *Slave Systems: Ancient and Modern,* edited by Enrico Dal Lago and Constantina Katsari, 3–31. Cambridge: Cambridge University Press, 2008.

Davis, Charles T., ed. *The Slave's Narrative.* New York: Oxford University Press, 1991.

de Certeau, Michel. *The Practice of Everyday Life.* Translated by Steven F. Rendall. Berkeley, CA: University of California Press, 1988.

Douglass, Frederick. *Life and Times of Frederick Douglass, Written by Himself.* 1892. Reprint, New York: Macmillan, 1962.

———. *Narrative of the Life of Frederick Douglass.* Boston: Anti-Slavery Office, 1845.

Dunbar, Paul Laurence. "'We Wear the Mask.'" In *The Complete Poems of Paul Laurence Dunbar.* New York: Dodd, Mead and Company. https://www.poetryfoundation.org/poems/44203/we-wear-the-mask. Accessed October 19, 2020.

Elaw, Zilpha. "Memoires of the Life, Religious Experience, Ministerial Travels, and Labours of Ms. Zilpha Elaw, an American Female of Colour; Together with Some Account of the Great Religious Revivals in America [Written by Herself]." In *Sisters of the Spirit,* edited by William L. Andrews, 49–160. Bloomington, IN: Indiana University Press, 1986.

Elliott, Susan M. (Elli). *Family Empires, Roman and Christian.* Volume 1: *Roman Family Empires.*Santa Rosa, CA: Polebridge, 2018.

Epictetus. *The Discourses as Reported by Arrian, the Manual, and Fragments.* 2 vols. Translated by Thomas Oldfather. LCL. 1925, 1928. Reprint, Cambridge: Harvard University Press, 1956, 1959.

Equiano, Olaudah. *The Interesting Narrative and Other Writings.* Rev ed. New York: Penguin, 2003.

Escott, Paul D. *Slavery Remembered: A Record of Twentieth-Century Slave Narratives.* Chapel Hill, NC: University of North Carolina, 1979.

Fairey, Emily. "Slavery in the Classical Utopia: A Comparative Study." PhD diss., City University of New York, 2006.

Feldstein, Stanley. *Once a Slave: The Slaves' View of Slavery*. New York: Morrow, 1971.

Flexsenhar, Michael III. *Christians in Caesar's Household: The Emperor's Slaves in the Makings of Christianity*. University Park, PA: University of Pennsylvania Press, 2019.

Flower, Harriet I. *The Dancing Lares and the Serpent in the Garden: Religion at the Roman Street Corner*. Princeton, NJ: Princeton University Press, 2017.

Frilingos, Chris. "'For My Child, Onesimus': Paul and Domestic Power in Philemon." *Journal of Biblical Literature* 119 (2000) 91–104.

Gamauf, Richard. "Slaves Doing Business: The Role of Roman Law in the Economy of a Roman Household." *European Review of History—Revue européenne d'histoire* 16 (2009) 331–46.

Garnsey, Peter. *Ideas of Slavery from Aristotle to Augustine*. W. B. Stanford Memorial Lectures. Cambridge: Cambridge University Press, 1996.

Gates, Henry Louis Jr. "How Many Slave Narratives Were There?" *The Root*. https://www.theroot.com/how-many-slave-narratives-were-there-17908 74721, accessed December 21, 2018.

Glancy, Jennifer E. "Bodies for Sale." SBL Annual Meeting, San Diego, November 23, 2019.

———. "The Sexual Use of Slaves: A Response to Kyle Harper on Jewish and Christian *Porneia*." *Journal of Biblical Literature* 134 (2015) 215–29.

———. *Slavery in Early Christianity*. Minneapolis: Fortress, 2006.

———. "Slaves at a Greco-Roman Banquet: A Response." In *Meals in the Early Christian World: Social Formation, Experimentation, and Conflict*, edited by Dennis E. Smith and Hal E. Taussig, 204–11. New York: Palgrave Macmillan, 2012.

Goodrich, John K. "From Slaves of Sin to Slaves of God: Reconsidering the Origin of Paul's Slavery Metaphor in Romans 6." *Bulletin for Biblical Research* 23.4 (2013) 509–30.

Goodspeed, Edgar J. *New Solutions of New Testament Problems*. Chicago: University of Chicago Press, 1927.

Hanson, Craig L. "A Greek Martyrdom Account of St. Onesimus." *Greek Orthodox Theological Review* 22 (1977) 319–39.

———. "The Passion of St. Onesimus of Colossae." http://www.ecclesia.gr/greek/press/theologia/material/1979_2_4_Hanson.pdf. Accessed May 29, 2020.

Harper, James. "Slaves and Freedmen in Imperial Rome." *American Journal of Philology* 93.2 (1972) 341–42.

Harper, Kyle. *Slavery in the Late Roman World, AD 275–425*. Cambridge: Cambridge University Press, 2011.

Harrill, J. Albert. *The Manumission of Slaves in Early Christianity*. Tübingen: Mohr, 1995.

———. *Slaves in the New Testament: Literary, Social, and Moral Dimensions*. Minneapolis: Fortress, 2006.

Harris, Murray J. *Slave of Christ: A New Testament Metaphor for Total Devotion to Christ*. Downers Grove, IL: InterVarsity, 1999.

Henson, Josiah. *Autobiography of the Rev. Josiah Henson ("Uncle Tom"), from 1798 to 1881*. London, ON: Schuyler, Smith & Co., 1881.

Hezser, Catherine. *Jewish Slavery in Antiquity*. Oxford: Oxford University Press, 2010.

Hodkinson, Stephen, and Dick Geary, eds. *Slaves and Religions in Graeco-Roman Antiquity and Modern Brazil*. Newcastle, UK: Cambridge Scholars, 2012.

Hodkinson, Stephen, and Dick Geary. "Introduction: Slaves and Religions: Historiographies, Ancient and Modern." In *Slaves and Religions in Graeco-Roman Antiquity and Modern* Brazil, edited by Stephen Hodkinson and Dick Geary, 1–33. Newcastle, UK: Cambridge Scholars, 2012.

Holmes, Michael W. *The Apostolic Fathers in English*. 3rd ed. Grand Rapids: Baker Academic, 2006.

Hurston, Zora Neale. *Barracoon: The Story of the Last "Black Cargo"*. San Francisco: Amistad, 2018.

Jacobs, Harriet, with Lydia Maria Child. *Incidents in the Life of a Slave Girl*. Boston: The Author, 1861.

Johnson, Matthew V. "Onesimus Speaks: Diagnosing the Hys/Terror of the Text," In *Onesimus Our Brother: Reading Religion, Race, and Culture in Philemon*, edited by Demetrius K. Williams and Matthew V. Johnson, 91–100. Minneapolis: Fortress, 2012.

Johnson, Walter. "On Agency." *Journal of Social History* 37.1 (2003) 113–24.

Jones, Ernest A. *Onesimus, the Run-Away Slave*. No loc.: First Book Library, 2004.

Joshel, Sandra R., and Lauren Hackworth Peterson. *The Material Life of Roman Slaves*. Cambridge: Cambridge University Press, 2014.

Joshel, Sandra R. *Slavery in the Roman World*. New York: Cambridge University Press, 2010.

Kartzow, Marianne Bjelland. *The Slave Metaphor and Gendered Enslavement in Early Christian Discourse: Double Trouble Embodied*. Routledge Studies in the Early Christian World. London: Routledge, 2018.

Keckley, Elizabeth. *Behind the Scenes, or, Thirty Years a Slave, and Four Years in the White House*. New York: G. W. Carleton, 1868.

Kirkegaard, Brad. "Placing Early Christianity as a Social Movement within Its Greco-Roman Context." *Journal of Lutheran Ethics*. https://www.elca.org/JLE/Articles/619.

Knox, John. *Philemon among the Letters of Paul: A New View of Its Place and Importance*. Rev. ed. Nashville, TN: Abingdon, 1959.

Krause, Jens-Uwe. *Gefängnisse im Römischen Reich*. Stuttgart: Steiner, 1995.

Kyrtatas, Dmitris K. "Slaves and Early Christianity: Serving God Rather Than Human Masters." *Post Augustum* 2 (2018) 1–9.

Lampe, Peter. *Christians at Rome in the First Two Centuries: From Paul to Valentinus*. London: Continuum, 2003.

Larsen, Lillian I. "Early Christian Meals and Slavery." In *Meals in the Early Christian World: Social Formation, Experimentation, and Conflict*, edited by Dennis E. Smith and Hal E. Taussig, 191–203. New York: Palgrave Macmillan, 2012.

Lewis, Lloyd A. "Philemon." In *True to Our Native Land: An African American New Testament Commentary*, edited by Brian K. Blount, 437–43. Minneapolis: Fortress, 2007.

Lightfoot, J. B. *Saint Paul's Epistles to Colossians and Philemon*. London: Macmillan, 1875.

Lim, Sung Uk. "The Otherness of Onesimus: Re-reading the Letter to Philemon from the Margins." *Theology Today* 73 (2016) 215–29.

MacDonald, Margaret Y. "Slavery, Sexuality and House Churches: A Reassessment of Colossians 3.18—4.1 in Light of New Research on the Roman Family." *New Testament Studies* 52 (2006) 94–113.

Marchal, Joseph A. "The Usefulness of an Onesimus." *Journal of Biblical Literature* 130 (2011) 749–70.

Martin, Dale B. *Slavery as Salvation: The Metaphor of Slavery in Early Christianity*. New Haven: Yale University Press, 2005.

McDowell, Markus. *Onesimus: A Novel of Christianity in the Roman Empire*. Los Angeles: Riversong, 2018.

McKeown, Niall. "Magic, Religion, and the Roman Slave: Resistance, Control, and Community." In *Slaves and Religions in Graeco-Roman Antiquity and Modern Brazil*, edited by Stephen Hodkinson and Dick Geary, 279–308. Newcastle, UK: Cambridge Scholars, 2012.

Nasrallah, Laura. *Archaeology and the Letters of Paul*. Oxford: Oxford University Press, 2019.

Nicklas, T. "Ancient Christian Care for Prisoners: First and Second Centuries." *Acta Theologica* 23 Supp. (2016) 49-65.

Nock, A. D. *Early Gentile Christianity and Its Hellenistic Background*. New York: Harper Torchbooks, 1957.

O'Loughlin, Thomas. *Discovering Saint Patrick*. Mahwah, NJ: Paulist, 2005.

Ogereau, Julien M. "A Survey of Κοινωνία and Its Cognates in Documentary Sources." *Novum Testamentum* 57 (2015) 275–94.

Oldfather, W. A. *Epictetus II. Books 3-4. The Enchiridion*. LCL 218. Cambridge, MA: Harvard University Press, 1928.

Osiek, Carolyn, and Margaret Y. MacDonald, with Janet H. Tulloch. "What We Do and Don't Know about Early Christian Families." In *A Companion to Families in the Greek and Roman Worlds*, edited by Beryl Rawson, 198–213. Oxford: Blackwell, 2011.

———. *A Woman's Place: House Churches in Earliest Christianity*. Minneapolis, MN: Fortress, 2006.

Patterson, Orlando. *Die the Long Day*. New York: Morrow, 1972.

———. *Slavery and Social Death: A Comparative Study*. 1982. Reprint, Cambridge, MA: Harvard University Press, 2018.

————. *The Sociology of Slavery: An Analysis of the Origins, Development and Structure of Negro Slave Society in Jamaica.* New York: Humanities, 1989.

Patterson, Stephen. *The Forgotten Creed: Christianity's Original Struggle against Bigotry, Slavery, and Sexism.* Oxford: Oxford University Press, 2018.

Peralta, Dan-el Padilla. "Slave Religiosity in the Roman Middle Republic." *Classical Antiquity* 36.2 (2017) 317–69.

Perkins, Pheme. "Philemon." In *The Women's Bible Commentary*, edited by Carol J. Newsom and Sharon H. Ringe, 362–63. Louisville, KY: Westminster John Knox, 1992.

Perry, Ben Edwin, trans. *Babrius and Phaedrus Fables.* LCL; Cambridge: Harvard University Press, 1965.

Petronius Arbiter. *The Satyricon, Complete.* Translated by W. C. Firebaugh. https://www.gutenberg.org/files/5225/5225-h/5225-h.htm#linkp070.

Pliny the Younger. *Letters.* Translated by William Melmoth; revised by F. C. T. Bosanquet. Harvard Classics. New York: Collier and Sons, 1909–14.

Potter, Mark. *Onesimus: The Prince and the Slave.* No loc.: Independently published, 2017.

Prince, Mary. *The History of Mary Prince, a West Indian Slave. Related by Herself. With a Supplement by the Editor. To Which Is Added, the Narrative of Asa-Asa, a Captured African.* London: F. Westley and A. H. Davis, 1831.

Punt, Jeremy. "Paul, Power and Philemon: 'Knowing Your Place.'" In *Postcolonial Biblical Interpretation: Reframing Paul*, 149–74. Studies in Theology and Religion. Leiden: Brill, 2015.

Raboteau, Albert J. *Slave Religion: The "Invisible Institution" in the Antebellum South.* 1978. Reprint, Oxford: Oxford University Press, 2004.

Roper, Moses. *Narrative of the Adventures and Escape of Moses Roper, from American Slavery.* Berwick-upon-Tweed, UK: Warder Office, 1848.

Seesengood, Robert. *Philemon: An Introduction and Study Guide.* London: Bloomsbury, 2017.

Seneca, L. Annaeus. *Minor Dialogs Together with the Dialog "On Clemency."* Translated by Aubrey Stewart. Bohn's Classical Library ed. London: George Bell, 1900.

Shaner, Katherine A. *Enslaved Leadership in Early Christianity.* New York: Oxford University Press, 2018.

Smith, Mitzi J. "Philemon." In *Women's Bible Commentary, Revised and Updated*, edited by Carol A. Newsom, Sharon H. Ringe, and Jacqueline E. Lapsley, 605–7. Louisville, KY: Westminster John Knox, 2012.

Smith, Timothy L. "Slavery and Theology: The Emergence of Black Christian Consciousness in Nineteenth Century America." *Church History* 41.4 (1972) 497–512.

Smith, Venture. *A Narrative of the Life and Adventures of Venture, a Native of Africa: But Resident above Sixty Years in the United States of America. Related by Himself.* New London, CT: C. Holt, 1798.

Standhartinger, Angela. "Aus der Welt eines Gefangenen: Die Kommuni-kationsstruktur des Philipperbriefs im Spiegel seiner Abfassungssituation." *Novum Testamentum* 55 (2013) 140–67.

Starobin, Robert S. *Blacks in Bondage: Letters of American Slaves.* 1988. Reprint, Princeton, NJ: Weiner, 1994.

Stevens, Charles E. *Anthony Burns, A History.* Boston: John P. Jewett, 1856.

Stowers, Stanley. "A Cult from Philadelphia: Oikos Religion or Cultic Association." In *The Early Church in Its Context: Essays in Honor of Everett Ferguson*, edited by Abraham J. Malherbe, Frederick W. Norris, and James W. Thompson, 287–301. NovSup. Leiden: Brill, 1998.

Tamez, Elsa, Cynthia Briggs Kittredge, Claire Miller Colombo, and Alicia J. Batten. *Philippians, Colossians, Philemon.* Wisdom Commentaries. Collegeville, MN: Liturgical, 2017.

Thompson, James W., and Bruce W. Longenecker. *Philippians and Philemon.* Paideia Commentaries on the New Testament. Grand Rapids: Baker, 2016.

Thompson, Marianne Meye. *Colossians and Philemon.* THNTC. Grand Rapids: Eerdmans, 2005.

Thurston, Bonnie B., and Judith M. Ryan. *Philippians & Philemon.* Sacra Pagina 10. Collegeville, MN: Liturgical, 2009.

Tiroyabone, Obusitswe. "Reading Philemon in the Postcolony: Exploring a Postcolonial Runaway Slave Hypothesis." *Acta Theologica* 24 (2016) 225–36.

Tolmie, D. François, ed. *Philemon in Perspective: Interpreting a Pauline Letter.* Berlin: De Gruyter, 2010.

Trainor, Michael. *Epaphras: Paul's Educator at Colossae.* Collegeville, MN: Liturgical, 2008.

Troelsch, Ernst. *The Social Teachings of the Christian Churches.* Vol. 1. London: Macmillan, 1931.

Truth, Sojourner, and Olive Gilbert. *Narrative of Sojourner Truth; a Bondswoman of Olden Time, Emancipated by the New York Legislature in the Early Part of the Present Century; with a History of Her Labors and Correspondence, Drawn from Her "Book of Life."* Boston: The Author, 1875.

Valentine, Katy E. "Slaves in the New Testament." Bible Odyssey. https://www.bibleodyssey.org/en/passages/related-articles/slavery-in-the-new-testament.

Wedow, Lindsey K. D. "'Servants, Obey Your Masters': Southern Representations of the Religious Lives of Slaves." *Gettysburg College Journal of the Civil War Era* 5 (2015) 1–27.

Welborn, L. L. *An End to Enmity: Paul and the "Wrongdoer" in 2 Corinthians.* Berlin: de Gruyter, 2011.

Whiston, William, trans. *Works of Flavius Josephus.* London: Nelson and Sons, 1883.

Williams, Demetrius K., and Matthew V. Johnson, eds. *Onesimus Our Brother: Reading Religion, Race, and Culture in Philemon.* Minneapolis: Fortress, 2012.

———. "'No Longer as a Slave': Reading the Interpretation History of Paul's Epistle to Philemon." In *Onesimus Our Brother: Reading Religion, Race, and Culture in Philemon*, edited by Demetrius K. Williams and Matthew V. Johnson, 11–45. Minneapolis: Fortress, 2012.

Williams, Heather Andrea. *Help Me to Find My People: The African American Search for Family Lost in Slavery*. Chapel Hill, NC: University of North Carolina Press, 2012.

Winter, Susan C. "Philemon." In *Searching the Scriptures: A Feminist Commentary*, edited by Elisabeth Schüssler Fiorenza, 301–12. New York: Crossroad, 1994.

Work Projects Administration. *The Voices from the Past: Hundreds of Testimonies by Former Slaves in One Volume*. Oxford: Madison & Adams Press, 2017.

Wrede, Henning. *Consecratio in Formam Deorum: vergöttlichte Privatpersonen in der römischen Kaiserzeit*. Mainz: Von Zabern, 1981.

# Index of Modern Authors

# Index of Subjects

# Index of Scriptures